THE ONLY HOPE FOR AMERICA

The Transforming Power
of the Gospel of Jesus Christ

LUIS PALAU

THE ONLY HOPE
FOR AMERICA

"Fired by an urgent passion to evangelize America in this generation, Luis Palau summons Christians to earnestly proclaim the Gospel's call to repent and believe in Jesus Christ."
> —RUSSELL CHANDLER
> *former religion writer*
> *The Los Angeles Times*

"With dynamic urgency Luis Palau pinpoints the causes that are driving individuals and entire societies into desperation in today's violent and divided world. Then he demonstrates that the Gospel of Jesus Christ is our only hope and that great numbers of people are turning to the Savior. I heartily recommend this book!"
> —KEITH J. HARDMAN
> *Professor*
> *Ursinus College*

"The churches of North America need a wake-up call to the priority of the evangelistic task; otherwise Christian presence and influence will be increasingly marginalized. Luis Palau presents a passionate plea for churches to work together to impact their city and nation."
> —REV. EDDIE GIBBS
> *Associate Rector for Discipleship*
> *All Saints' Parish, Beverly Hills, CA*

"Luis Palau is one of God's most gifted evangelists in the world today, and a man for whom I have the greatest possible love and respect."
> —BILLY GRAHAM
> *Evangelist*

"A Luis Palau crusade is one of the most Spirit-led crusades we have in the world today—thoroughly organized and prepared, biblically sound, and Christ-centered. Dr. Palau's Hispanic background gives us the opportunity to demonstrate that the Gospel of Jesus Christ knows no ethnic bounds as diverse cultures come together to hear the Gospel clearly preached and the challenge given to trust Christ."
> —E. V. HILL
> *Senior Pastor*
> *Mount Zion Missionary Baptist Church, Los Angeles*

"Luis Palau is a voice to which this generation must listen, because he shares God's heart for spiritual awakening in the churches, and for the multitudes who are still outside of His kingdom. Thank God that millions are listening!"

—DAVID BRYANT
Founder and President
Concerts of Prayer International

"There are many practical reasons for supporting the ministry of Luis Palau: his fidelity to the truth, his constancy of passion for the lost, and his integrity in personal life—these are sufficient to begin. But the all-encompassing fact that compels my belief in Luis and the outreach of the Palau Evangelistic Association is the evidence of God's sovereign choice to anoint and use this man mightily at this crucial juncture in church history."

—JACK W. HAYFORD
Senior Pastor
The Church on the Way, Van Nuys, CA

"I am so encouraged by the Palau Association's emphasis on pre-crusade prayer and the power of God. I had the privilege of training Christians in prayer and intercession for the Luis Palau and Billy Graham crusades in England the results were incredible. Prayer is the   strength of Luis Palau."

—EVELYN CHRISTENSON
Evelyn Christenson Ministries

"I have known dear brother Luis Palau for many years and have the highest appreciation for him personally and his integrity. The Spirit of God is upon this man."

—KENNETH N. TAYLOR
Chairman of the Board
Tyndale House Publishers

"Luis Palau stands out as a gifted evangelist who crosses cultural lines to speak to men and women about Jesus Christ. Wherever I have traveled in the United States or beyond its borders, I have met those who have been touched and transformed by the good news about Jesus Christ as it was presented to them by Mr. Palau. We're grateful to God for this gifted servant."

—DR. HADDON ROBINSON
Professor
Gordon-Conwell Theological Seminary

THE ONLY HOPE FOR AMERICA

The Transforming Power of the Gospel of Jesus Christ

LUIS PALAU

with MIKE UMLANDT

CROSSWAY BOOKS • WHEATON, ILLINOIS
A DIVISION OF GOOD NEWS PUBLISHERS

Art Direction/Design: Cindy Kiple

First printing, 1996

Printed in the United States of America

Library of Congress Cataloging-in-Publication Data
Palau, Luis
  The only hope for America: the transforming power of the Gospel of Jesus Christ / Luis Palau with Mike Umlandt.
    p. cm.
ISBN 0-89107-882-7
  Includes bibliographical references.
  1. Evangelistic work--United States. 2. Palau, Luis, 1934-
3. Revivals—United States. 4. United States—Moral conditions.
5. United States—Church history—20th century. I. Umlandt, Mike.
II. Title.
BV3790.P24 1996
269'.2'0973—dc20   95-44520

04		03		02		01		00		99		98		97		96
15	14	13	12	11	10	9	8	7	6	5	4	3	2	1

CONTENTS

INTRODUCTION

Recently a woman and her husband, professing Christians, asked me why I am an evangelist. "I long to see people changed by Jesus Christ," I replied. "That's my greatest source of satisfaction."

She responded, "In my whole life I've never seen a person actually changed by Jesus Christ."

Her comment first touched my conscience. How changed am I by Jesus Christ? How different am I from my unchurched, unconverted neighbors?

Then I wanted to tell her about thousands of people I know whose lives have been dramatically changed: a drug dealer who once made thousands of dollars a week now gladly living for Christ while working a regular job; adulterous husbands and wives who now honor their marriage vows; lonely, withdrawn teenagers who now can't stop talking about Jesus at home and school; drug-addicted celebrities who now testify of deliverance and host Bible studies in their homes.

In the past three years I've even seen my son Andrew

change right in front of my eyes after he finally repented and gave his life to the Lord.

Andrew is my third of four sons, born in Cali, Colombia, in 1966 while my wife, Pat, and I were first-term missionary-evangelists with Overseas Crusades. After graduating from the University of Oregon, Andrew moved to Boston where, as a confident young man, he began his climb up the corporate ladder. But it wasn't his distance from home that troubled my heart; it was his distance from the Lord.

Like our other sons, Andrew had prayed to invite Jesus to come into his heart when he was a child. Since high school, however, he had had little interest in the Bible and church. "Fraternity life" ruled in college, where Andrew followed the path of least resistance. God occasionally stepped in but could not fit in.

Now living on the other side of the continent, Andrew adopted a secular lifestyle with secular values. Painful as it was, Pat and I had to accept what we had counseled other parents. Just because Andrew was brought up in Sunday school, had memorized Scripture verses, was baptized, could talk the language, and even respected and defended the Gospel as truth, that did not mean he was truly converted. Conversion is essential for everyone, whether born into a pagan family or a family that seeks to honor Jesus Christ in everything they do.

Andrew was extremely respectful of his parents, always courteous and kind to us, a tremendous son who never blasphemed the Gospel, but his life denied a personal conversion experience with the Lord Jesus Christ.

For many years my heart carried this burdensome weight. The moments right before I stand to preach the Gospel of Jesus Christ to a crowd of thousands hold a mixture of emotions. There's thankfulness to God for granting me another harvest-time opportunity. There's anticipation and joy, knowing that God is patiently at work in many hearts, "not wanting anyone to perish, but everyone to come to repentance" (2 Peter 3:9). And until a few years ago there was sadness, because in these moments the thoughts of this father would almost always turn to Andrew. And so often, as I sat on the platform and prayed, "Lord, may many come forward to confess Christ," I'd be thinking, *There's no greater joy than this . . . but what about Andrew? How can my joy be complete until Andrew stands here as one who walks with Christ?*

Andrew's rebellion was a painful lesson. Because one of my sons—whom I did my very best to channel into the ways of Christ—resisted conversion, I was kept from certain aspects of arrogance and from self-righteousness. The Gospel is all of mercy, all of grace. I was not so charming and wonderful as to cause Andrew to walk as a saint and never besmirch the name of Christ.

I could do no more than cling to God's promise to Israel: "All your sons will be taught by the Lord, and great will be your children's peace" (Isaiah 54:13). I prayed that verse many times through the years for all of my sons.

Three years ago, all glory to God, Andrew returned to the Lord. Pat and I had invited him to come with us to Jamaica for the "Say Yes to Jesus" crusade. There he met Robert Levy, the crusade's finance chairman, his son Chris, and his daughter Wendy. Their energetic commitment to Christ convicted Andrew of his harmful waywardness. Though his good intentions to change subsequently failed, weeks later another visit to Jamaica (to see Wendy) led to what Andrew calls "some serious repenting."

Was it first-time repentance and genuine belief? Was it a recommitment to Christ? To me it doesn't matter whether my son was converted as a child or at age twenty-seven. My joy is that now both of us know that the Spirit of God is living in him. Andrew is born of God and bearing the fruit of sonship, being conformed to the likeness of the Lord Jesus Christ.[1] He recently completed graduate studies at Multnomah Biblical Seminary and is serving the Lord with me. Andrew frequently speaks to young people at high schools and colleges during our team's evangelistic crusades.

I now preach the Gospel with ever more conviction. The resurrected Christ has power to change America, where 80 percent of the people claim to be Christians, but few live any differently from pagans or atheists, as though God has no claim on their lives. Their hearts have not been changed, and unless Jesus Christ changes their hearts, they never will be any different from those outside the Christian faith.

America needs to be evangelized like never before. Billy Graham once said, "It's either back to the Bible or back to the jungle." The jungle is creeping up on the United States.

Theologian Carl F. H. Henry put it this way: "The barbarians are coming." Dr. Henry could see that without a wave of evangelization that converts hundreds of thousands of people to Jesus Christ, barbarians are going to take over the land. Not foreigners, but our own unrepentant children and grandchildren.

The problem is in the heart, not just the outward behavior that so alarms and frightens God-fearing Americans. God says, "The heart is deceitful above all things, and desperately wicked" (Jeremiah 17:9 KJV). What's needed is not more good advice dished out in the newspaper and on television, but the Good News, "the power of God for the salvation of everyone who believes" (Romans 1:16).

Political campaigns, family counseling, and education do nothing about the condition of human depravity. Unless there's a change of heart, nothing's happened to change a person. And unless millions of hearts are changed, little has happened to change America. Dr. Henry says, "The ideal way to transform a sinful society is not political compulsion but spiritual transformation—that is, evangelistic proclamation and regeneration."

If we proclaim the Gospel with all the vigor of the Holy Spirit, I'm convinced hundreds of thousands, if not millions, of Americans will listen and trust Jesus Christ for salvation. That's the only hope for America.

$\underline{1}$

THE CHURCH'S (FORGOTTEN) NUMBER ONE PRIORITY

Then Jesus came to them and said, "All authority
in heaven and on earth has been given to me.
Therefore go and make disciples of all nations,
baptizing them in the name of the Father and of
the Son and of the Holy Spirit, and teaching them
to obey everything I have commanded you.
And surely I am with you always, to the very
end of the age."

— Matthew 28:18-20

_1_

A WHILE BACK THE MISSIONS COMMITTEE of a supporting church wrote to let our evangelistic association know they were cutting their support of us by 50 percent. Paraphrased, the letter said, "We love you. We think the world of you. But giving is down. May God provide for your needs." Nothing unusual—I'm sure every missions organization gets letters like this.

In the same envelope, however, was the church's weekly bulletin. One announcement caught my attention: "The pastor and twenty men in the church will be leaving this week with their wives for a golf tournament in the Bahamas. Pray for them."

Now I'm all for golf tournaments. Golf is a fine game. And these twenty-one couples can spend their money any way they want. But I confess it bothered me to know that in this church hitting and chasing a little white ball seems to be a greater priority than evangelistic ministry.

"The work of conversion is the first and great thing we must drive at; after this we must labour with all our might," said Charles H. Spurgeon, the great nineteenth-century British preacher. And John Wesley reminded preachers, "You have nothing to do but to save souls."

I believe evangelism is the main work of the church of Jesus Christ. I've debated that point with many good friends, including one of my mentors, who believed that if you build up the church and worship right on Sunday morning, emphasizing solid biblical exposition, the people automatically will give witness to their faith at work and around the community come Monday.

At the World Congress on Evangelism in Berlin in 1966, one of evangelical Christianity's most respected statesmen said, "Evangelism happens when the people of God walk with God."

But thirty years of experience tell me it doesn't work that way. I know great worshiping people who just plain don't share their faith and godly men and women for whom evangelism never "happens." If evangelism happened naturally, the Lord wouldn't have commanded it repeatedly.

NOTHING IS
MORE IMPORTANT

Evangelism is a chosen act of obedience to God's revealed will. It is the highest, most important act of obedience for a Christian, because there is nothing more important to God, "who wants all men to be saved" (1 Timothy 2:4). "The Lord . . . is patient with you, not wanting anyone to perish, but everyone to come to repentance" (2 Peter 3:9).

Jesus made His mission very plain: "For the Son of Man came to seek and to save what was lost" (Luke 19:10). We know His final command to "go and make disciples of all nations" (Matthew 28:19) as the Great Commission, not the great suggestion.

It's a commission largely ignored today.[1] There are pockets of action, thank God, but evangelism isn't a priority, let alone *the* priority, for thousands of churches and Christians in America. Since 1990, when our association began to focus much of our ministry helping to re-evangelize America, my team and I have led evangelistic crusades in more than a dozen U.S. cities. In each one evangelism has been warfare, and too many of its most vehement opponents have been Christians. It takes an excruciating effort to persuade many Christians just to come to an evangelistic meeting, let alone to pray for unsaved friends, practice friendship evangelism, and invite friends to come along to hear the Gospel in a quality setting.

I understand that the method—crusade evangelism—is sometimes the focus of some churches' misguided opposition, not evangelism itself. But in the months of preparation, prayer, and training for a crusade in a city, visiting scores of churches and getting to know their pastors, our team members discover that most churches devote very little time to evangelism of *any* kind.

Sometimes opposition to a particular method of evangelism cloaks defensiveness about the content of the Gospel. Embarrassed about the Gospel, some churchmen want to keep the light under a bushel.

In reality, arguing against a method is almost always a smoke screen for inaction. As D. L. Moody, the great nineteenth-century evangelist, told one critic who didn't approve of his mass evangelism methods, "I don't like them too much myself. What methods do *you* use?" When the critic indicated he didn't use any evangelistic tools or activities, Moody said, "Well, I like the way I do it better than the way you don't."

PLEASE EXCUSE ME

Still, critics and nonparticipants abound. Here's a list of the most common excuses we hear for not getting involved in a citywide evangelistic crusade:

- •"We have our own evangelistic programs." *Fine. Let's work together and extend the kingdom!*

- •"We are too busy." *But are you about the Lord's most important work?*

- •"The deacons won't let our church get involved." *Why not? Let's talk and pray about it.*

- •"We don't believe in evangelism." *What exactly do you believe? Is your church a Christian church?*

- •"We don't believe in your form of evangelism." *Crusade evangelism encompasses a wide variety of methods. Which do you prefer?*

- •"We don't want to make a show of evangelism." *Agreed. Let's work together to exalt Jesus Christ, not the event or the evangelists.*

- •"Crusade decision-makers never go on with the Lord." *Actually, in-depth research of several of our crusades has shown that more than 70 percent are active members of a local church six months after the crusades.*[2]

- •"You are not contemporary enough." *I suppose it depends on which crusade event you attend.*

- •"You are too contemporary." *Please stay home on youth night.*

- •"Crusades don't work anymore." *George Barna, Russell Chandler, C. Peter Wagner, and others have said that perhaps the greatest crusades in American history are yet ahead.*

- •"Our church is already full—we don't have room for any more." *Great! Let's work together and help fill other churches.*

•"Right now our church is into prayer ministry." *Are you praying by name each day for your unsaved neighbors, relatives, and friends? Together let's tell them the Gospel.*

•"We have to build up our saints first before we can do evangelism." *What better way to disciple them than by getting them actively involved in helping fulfill the Great Commission? According to the Apostle Paul, God uses the Gospel and the proclamation of Jesus Christ to "establish" believers (Romans 16:25).*

•"We are in the middle of a building project." *Great! Let's work together to build God's kingdom at the same time and fill up your church with new babes in Christ.*

George Barna issues a wake-up call to Christians to "get into the game and share the good news, now!"[3] He adds, "How ironic that during this period of swelling need for the proclamation of the Gospel and the healing powers of the Church, the ranks of the messengers have dissipated to anemic proportions."[4]

STIMULATE TO WITNESS

The Luis Palau Evangelistic Association's mission is not only to win as many people as possible to Jesus Christ, but also to stimulate, train, and mobilize the church to continuous, effective evangelism, follow-up, and church growth. A crusade helps to renew churches to be more effective in their evangelistic ministries. If they don't have an evangelism program, we want to help them get one going. If they have one that's not working well, we want to help infuse it with power. And if they have a dynamic program, we hope to give it a boost of energy and join with them in teaching others how to win people to Christ.

Maranatha Bible Church in Grand Rapids, Michigan, where our team held a crusade recently, serves as an example. The pastor, John Campbell, enthusiastically brought the crusade opportunity before his board. It elicited much debate, which centered on the many denominations involved. But the vote was six in favor, five opposed.

Though disheartened that the vote was so close, the pastor challenged all of the elders and deacons to get involved in some aspect of the crusade, and they did. After the crusade, there was unanimous agreement that it was an overwhelming blessing for everyone in the congregation. Each board member who was previously opposed to involvement had become a crusade supporter. One elder praised the training. Another was impressed with the spirit of oneness and cooperation among people from different denominations.

One man said his attitude changed during the friendship evangelism training, particularly when another man in the church stood up and reported that after the first session he was burdened to pray for and share the Gospel with a seriously ill co-worker. Two days later he led his co-worker to Christ.

"God has changed our hearts," Pastor Campbell says. "Our church board and our congregation have more compassion for the lost than they ever had before. God used our involvement in the crusade as a springboard to move our church's focus from an inward one to an outward one. They saw God working in and through this crusade to bring people to salvation in His Son, and it has changed us permanently. Thank God."

SINGLE-MINDED RESCUERS

Remember Captain Scott O'Grady, the air force F-16 pilot who evaded capture in Bosnia after being shot down in 1995? After his dramatic rescue, my friend Jim Reapsome compared the mission of the church to the marines' heroism. Jim bemoaned many churches' wasted energy in battles over peripheral matters, like praise choruses versus traditional hymns.

"The devil is having a field day, because every such intramural fight is a gain for his schemes to keep us from doing our primary mission—breaking down the walls of his kingdom of darkness and rescuing people for God's kingdom of light," he wrote. The marines who rescued Captain O'Grady "did not sit around and argue about which arrangement of the Marine Corps hymn to sing. They pursued a single mission—rescue a downed pilot—and they allowed nothing to sidetrack them."

Jim concluded, "As the old saying goes, we must keep the main thing the main thing, which is to throw life lines of hope and peace to people trampled and overcome by despair."[5]

In today's church there simply isn't a conviction to get out the simple, unadorned Gospel of John 3:16-18 and 1 Corinthians 15:1-3. I easily get emotional when I think about that gospel message, which comes directly from the heart of God. Every time we preach, we must let people know that God loves them. He is actively looking for them.

Thanks to missionaries who brought that message to South America, both my father and mother are in heaven. My father died of a sudden, severe illness when he was only thirty-four years old. Shortly before he died, struggling to breathe, he sat up in bed and began to sing, "'Bright crowns up there, bright crowns for you and me.'" Then he fell back on his pillow and said, "I'm going to be with Jesus, which is far better." Two years ago, my mother joined him in heaven. Thank God for the gospel message and for the missionaries who sacrificially brought it to us and with it the assurance of eternal life (John 10:28)!

DESPERATE TO PERSUADE

In today's church there's no urgency to evangelize partly because we don't deeply believe the lost are really lost. We don't out-and-out deny it because that would sound heretical, but we don't embrace it, because if we did, we'd be much more *desperate* to persuade lost and dying people to turn to Christ.

"Each man's life is but a breath" (Psalm 39:5), and then we enter eternity—either eternal joy with God in heaven or eternal torment in hell. "God keeps no halfway house," Evangelist Billy Sunday preached. "It's either heaven or hell for you and me."

"The moment a soul drops the body and stands naked before God, it cannot but know what its portion will be to all eternity," John Wesley said. "It will have full in its view, either everlasting joy, or everlasting torment."

A friend of mine whose mother is dying without Christ doesn't seem to feel the same despair that I feel, and she's not my mother. I know my friend cares, but if my mother were dying without Christ, I think I'd spend every day on my knees by her bed until she surrendered to the Savior.

One of my team members, David Jones, received word at our Portland office that his father-in-law had only hours to live in a Minnesota hospital halfway across the country. For years Mr. Stevens had refused to listen to his daughter's and David's appeals to give his life to Christ. He was mad at God because his wife had died forty years earlier of cancer.

David rushed home, phoned the hospital room, and asked a nurse to hold the phone to his father-in-law's ear. "Dad, you've got only a few hours to live," he said. "Soon you're going to face your Creator. Isn't it time to get things right with the Lord?"

Despite the tubes in his mouth and nose, the old fellow managed to speak. "Yes," he said.

David quickly went through the Four Spiritual Laws and asked, "Would you like to receive Christ?"

Mr. Stevens prayed aloud with David, confessing his sin and trusting Jesus Christ. Overjoyed that her dad would be with the Lord, Gayle promised her husband, "You don't ever have to buy me another gift, for no gift can match knowing I'll see Daddy again in heaven."

George Barna tells about a Bill Hybels sermon on the rich man and Lazarus. Chills ran down his spine, Mr. Barna says, as Pastor Hybels passionately read the plaintive cry of the rich man, who was in torment in hell, to Abraham: "I beg you, father, send Lazarus to my father's house, for I have five brothers. Let him warn them, so that they will not also come to this place of torment" (Luke 16:27-28).

"To this day, more than a decade later, I recall that lesson and the horror that filled me as I realized, perhaps for the first time, how horrific a life in hell would be, how significant the death of Christ had been for me, and just how imperative it is to use every resource available to share the real truth about life, death, sin, and grace with every person I know."[6]

Mr. Barna could not sleep that night, knowing that many friends and family members would join Lazarus in eternal torment unless somebody told them the Gospel of grace in Jesus Christ. He knew the "somebody" was meant to be him. His life as an "evangelizer" hasn't been the same since.

All of us could use a few restless nights. Let's pray for restless nights, for burning tears, for sobs of compassion.

After all, the number one responsibility of a Christian is not to retire young in order to spend endless hours chasing a little white ball. If only people could get as excited about building the kingdom of God as they do about their handicap on the golf course.

Yes, evangelism is spiritual warfare. In evangelism we engage Satan nose to nose and try to steal his prey. So we should expect a few doors slammed in our face and more severe attacks on us and on our families.

But there's near ecstatic joy in obeying the Lord. A few inconveniences such as cynicism, rejection, yes, even imprisonment only seemed to heighten the happiness of Jesus' first-century followers.

"As soon as ever you have won a soul, you won't care about any of the other things," Moody said.

To be giving out the Gospel, leading people into the eternal kingdom of God Almighty—I can never have more fun. There's no greater thrill. Give evangelism all you've got. This life is your only chance.

TO PONDER

1. Read Matthew 28:18-20, which opens this chapter, again. What is the focus of the Great Commission? When did Jesus give this commission? To whom? For how long? For what purpose?

2. Early in this chapter, I say, "I believe evangelism is the main work of the church of Jesus Christ." What do you believe and why? As Christians, do we have a common ground upon which we can discuss this issue and truly come to a consensus?

3. "Evangelism is a chosen act of obedience to God's revealed will. It is the highest, most important act of obedience for a Christian, because there is nothing more

important to God." How does the Lord expect you and me to help fulfill the Great Commission in this generation? If I have the gift of evangelism and you don't feel you do, does that change God's expectations? In what way?

4. "There are pockets of action, thank God, but evangelism isn't a priority, let alone *the* priority, for thousands of churches and Christians in America." What priority does your church give to evangelism overseas? In this country? In your community? What priority do you yourself give to evangelism?

5. "In today's church there simply isn't a conviction to get out the simple, unadorned Gospel of John 3:16-18 and 1 Corinthians 15:1-3." When was the last time you heard the "simple, unadorned Gospel" proclaimed? When was the last time you saw someone embrace that message and publicly profess his or her faith in Jesus Christ?

6. "In today's church there's no urgency to evangelize, partly because we don't believe the lost are really lost." Why is that? Are we embarrassed about hell? Are we skeptical of the Scripture's teachings about eternity? What is at stake?

7. "Give evangelism all you've got. This life is your only chance." What is the down side if we get serious about helping fulfill the Great Commission? What is the up side? Which matters more to you?

2

CHANGING AMERICA FROM THE INSIDE OUT

Therefore, if anyone is in Christ, he is a new creation; the old has gone, the new has come!
— 2 Corinthians 5:17

2

WHEN VICTOR CALLED, he was a man on the run, desperate, lonely, with a gun and two bullets. He would need only one. . . .

For fifteen years Victor moved with the Mexican Mafia, dealing drugs in east Los Angeles. He earned ten thousand dollars a week. Sometimes fifteen thousand. But his wife and three children left him. One brother was in prison. Two friends and a cousin were dead.

"You'd better get out of here 'cause you're not doin' nothin' with your life," his father counseled. "You'll just end up like your cousin."

Victor took his father's advice and boarded a bus to Tulsa. Six months later, with no friends, no steady job, and mounting pressure to return to Los Angeles, Victor was ready to end his life.

October 13. The gun lay on a table in his apartment, but

he couldn't find the bullets. Nervously surfing through channels on TV, he stopped to listen to *Night Talk,* our call-in counseling program broadcast each evening that week during the Greater Tulsa Crusade. Thinking I was a psychologist, Victor called the number on the screen. By the time he was put through to me on the air, Victor had watched as I prayed with two others who had called.

"I just want to know, maybe you think God might be able to help me?" he asked. And he told me his story. My heart melted with compassion. I advised him to change his phone number to stop the calls from old buddies, and I promised to put him in touch with Christian men his age who could encourage him and counter the lures to L.A.

Most of all, he needed the Lord. "Tonight, Victor, are you ready to open your heart to Christ?" I asked.

"Do you think He could help me?"

"Absolutely. The Lord wants to come into your life. Christ died on the cross for you, Victor. He took away all the guilt and shame of the things you've done and paid the punishment that you and I deserve. If the law caught up with you for dealing drugs, they would come down hard. The law hasn't caught you, but the Lord has. Instead of nailing you, the Lord says, 'Victor, I love you.'

"Christ is calling you, knocking at the door of your heart. If you say, 'Yes, Lord Jesus, I don't understand it all, but I want You to come into my life,' you're going to see a change that you won't believe. In a year you'll be a different man, filled with joy and contentment. You'll have different goals in life, different dreams. You'll have power to overcome temptation. Christ will really change your life, but you must open your heart to Him, and I'd like to help you do that."

In the next moments, Victor received Christ as his Savior. He threw his gun into the river the next day, and that evening he came with one of our team members to the crusade rally, saying he felt like a new man.

"Victor, you *are* a new man," I assured him as the Convention Center crowd welcomed him with rousing applause.

Several months later, Victor moved again—to a place far from Los Angeles. He found steady work in landscaping and accountable fellowship at a good church. Though his wife doesn't believe he's a changed man and refuses to restore their marriage, Victor is a new creation in Christ.

"I haven't carried a gun in a year," he told our team members when he visited the Palau Association's Center for World Evangelism. "I'm working, which I have never really done before. I read the Bible and pray—I just sit down and talk to God. If people think I'm crazy, I don't care. . . . I don't care if they laugh at me. I used to get angry. If somebody even looked at me bad, I'd have beat him up. There are times when I feel like giving up, and then I think, *No, I've gone too far. Don't give up now.* I know God is with me."

EVANGELISM IS THE BEST SOCIAL ACTION

A Stanford University professor once challenged me: "Palau, how can you go to country after country where people have so many economic and social problems and preach about the resurrected Christ? Can't you do something more practical for them?"

"There isn't a better way to help them," I replied. "The people of this world create the problems of this world. If we can lead them to Christ, we will create a climate for other positive, practical changes to take place."

The professor was right, of course, that we live in a world

full of immense problems—a world weighed down by violence, disease, injustice, poverty, oppression, and addiction.

But as Christians, we can help alleviate such misery. We are called to serve as Jesus Christ served, caring for widows and children, feeding the hungry, healing the sick, breaking the chains of injustice—and leading people to receive the gift of life in Jesus Christ. Through His death and resurrection, Jesus is our hope that lives can change here and now and for eternity.

Today, if the Stanford professor still disputes the power of the Gospel, I'd love to introduce him to Victor—and to Victor's father, two older brothers, and a sister who have received Christ since Victor's conversion.

How can Christians in America possibly question the power of the Gospel to change lives? In fact, most of us do, but not by a direct challenge. Instead, our doubt shows up in our priorities, in our agendas to change society. There's little enthusiasm for evangelism. Political action, yes. Public protest, yes. Openly and vigorously winning souls, no. That's why we're not using the Gospel as a tool to change America. We're not going for conversions.

CHANGED IN AN INSTANT

"Know what I miss in this day of high technology? Good old salvation stories," says Jerry Jenkins, author of numerous books.[1]

I, too, love those old-fashioned testimonies that show God's power to change a life instantaneously. Near the end of five weeks of evangelistic campaigns in Wales several years ago, an old farmer named Peter handed me a card. "Thanks, Luis," it said. "I've given up drinking half a bottle of whiskey a day." Several weeks earlier Peter had been converted.

"Do you ever get tempted now when you smell alcohol?" I asked him. "Does it get to you?"

"I can't stand the smell of the stuff," Peter replied. "You said Christ could liberate me instantly, and He did."

Billy Sunday was a baseball player with the Chicago White Sox in 1887 when he was converted. His retelling of the story became one of the evangelist's most memorable messages:

"Twenty-seven years ago I walked down a street in Chicago in company with some ball players who were famous in this world—some of them are dead now—and we went into a saloon. It was Sunday afternoon, and we got tanked up and then went and sat down on a corner. . . . Across the street a company of men and women were playing on instruments— horns, flutes, and slide trombones—and the others were singing the gospel hymns that I used to hear my mother sing back in the log cabin in Iowa and back in the old church where I used to go to Sunday school.

"God painted on the canvas of my recollection and memory a vivid picture of the scenes of other days and other faces. Many have long since turned to dust. I sobbed and sobbed, and a young man stepped out and said, 'We are going down to the Pacific Garden Mission. Won't you come down to the mission? I am sure you will enjoy it. You can hear drunkards tell how they have been saved and girls tell how they have been saved from the red-light district.'

"I arose and said to the boys, 'I'm through. I am going to Jesus Christ. We've come to the parting of the ways.' Some of them laughed and some of them mocked me; one of them gave me encouragement; others never said a word.

"I turned and left that little group on the corner and walked to the little mission and fell on my knees and staggered out of sin and into the arms of the Saviour."[2]

Evangelism is the deepest, most profound, and most important social action in the world. It gives us hope in otherwise hopeless situations because God is stepping into hearts and lives. And what a difference that makes!

A REVOLUTIONARY LESSON

I learned this early in my ministry. I was doing a live call-in counseling program in the HCJB-TV studios in Quito, Ecuador, and had just prayed with a woman named Ruth, who confessed her immorality and received Jesus Christ as Savior. The next call was brief. A high-pitched, squeaky voice requested an appointment the next day at 9:30.

Right on time the next morning, a small woman walked through the gates of the HCJB property, followed closely by two huge men. As she entered the office, her eyes traveled to every corner before she finally sat down.

"You pastors and priests," she began with disgust. "You are a bunch of thieves and liars and crooks. All you want is to deceive people; all you want is money!"

She went on that way for more than twenty minutes, swearing all the while and smoking every last bit from each cigarette she lit.

I prayed silently, *Lord, how shall I handle this?* Seemingly exhausted, she finally slumped in her chair.

"Madam," I began, "is there anything I can do for you? How can I help you?"

She took her cigarette from her lips and sat staring at me for an instant; then she broke into uncontrollable sobs. When she was composed and could speak again, the edge was gone from her voice. "You know," she said, "in the thirty-eight years I have lived, you are the first person who has ever asked me if he could help me."

"What is your name?" I asked.

She was suddenly hard again. "Why do you want to know my name?"

"Well, you've said a lot of things here, and I don't even know you. I just want to know how to address you."

"My name is Maria Benitez-Perez," she said triumphantly. I recognized the name as that of a large family of wealth and influence. "I am the female secretary of the Communist Party in Ecuador. I am a Marxist-Leninist, and I am a materialist. I don't believe in God."

With that she took off on another breathless tirade against me, all preachers and priests, and the church.

"Why did you come here?" I broke in. "Just to insult me?"

For the next three hours, she told me her story. Maria had left home and run away from a religious school as a rebellious teenager. The Communists befriended her, and she became a party leader.

I let her talk, wondering when her first sign of vulnerability would surface.

"When my mother died, and the bishop came to officiate at the ceremony, I mocked him while my mother's body lay there in the casket," she said. "And I've always felt a little guilty about that, even though I don't believe in God, of course."

Every time she got onto the subject of God, she became enraged. But just as often, she would return to her mother's funeral.

"Hey, Palau," she said, "supposing there is a God—which there isn't—but just supposing there is—do you think He would receive a woman like me?"

I had read once that, when dealing with a professed atheist, the best approach is to take one truth from the Bible and stay with it. *What verse suits her?* I wondered. The Lord gave me Hebrews 10:17.

"Look, Maria, don't worry about what I think. Look at what God thinks." I opened to the verse and turned the Bible so she could see.

"I don't believe in the Bible. . . ."

"But we're just supposing there's a God, right? Let's just suppose this is His Word. He says, 'Their sins and iniquities I will remember no more.'"

She waited, as if there had to be more. "But listen, I've been an adulteress, married three times, and in bed with a lot of men."

I said, "'Their sins and iniquities I will remember no more.'"

"But I haven't told you half my story. I stabbed a comrade who later committed suicide."

"'Their sins and iniquities I will remember no more.'"

"I've led student riots where people were killed."

"'Their sins and iniquities I will remember no more.'"

Seventeen times I responded to Maria's objections and confessions with that verse. "Would you like Christ to forgive all that you've told me about and all the rest that I don't even know?" I asked.

"He can't do it," she said.

"You want to try it?"

"It would be a miracle."

"Take a step of faith. Invite Him into your life and try Him. See what will happen."

Maria stared at me for a long moment and then bowed her head. "All right," she whispered.

I led her in a simple prayer of decision, confessing her sins, asking forgiveness, and receiving Jesus Christ.

She returned a week later to tell me she was reading the

Bible. A missionary from HCJB agreed to follow her up, but I was not prepared for what I would encounter when I saw Maria again in January. Her face was a mess of purple blotches and bruises. Several of her front teeth were missing.

At a meeting of all the Communist leaders of the country, she told them, "I am no longer an atheist. I believe in God and in Jesus Christ. I am resigning from the party, and I don't want to have anything more to do with it. We are all a bunch of liars. We deceive people when we tell them there is no God."

A few days later, four of Maria's former comrades attacked her and smashed her face. She was forced to hide out in the basements of churches and in the homes of missionaries.

"There's going to be a revolution in June," she told me matter-of-factly. "We've had it all planned for months." Students and agitators would cause a disturbance in the streets, luring out the army, which would then be attacked and overthrown. The military junta would be forced to leave the country, and the chairman of the Communist Party for Ecuador would come out of hiding in Colombia and take over the country.

Maria remained on the run until June, but the Marxists' network of spies tracked her down. Rather than letting them take her, however, she talked her four captors into retreating to her father's farm in the Ecuadorean interior, where they could rest and read a few Christian books she had chosen for them.

On the morning of the revolution, the Communist Party leader came out of Colombia to talk to Maria, his longtime friend. "Maria, why did you become a Christian?"

"Because I believe in God and in Jesus Christ, and my faith has changed my life."

"You know," he said, "while hiding out, I have been listening to HCJB radio on shortwave, and those Christians— they almost have me believing there is a God!"

"There is!" she said. "Why don't you become a

Christian and get out of this business? Look at all the lives we've ruined. Here, take this Bible and this book (*Peace with God* by Billy Graham). You can go to my father's farm and read them."

He accepted her offer. Later that morning, the disturbance that was supposed to trigger revolution fizzled into chaos because the leaders were off on a farm, reading.

Was Maria's conversion to Christ effective social action? Her changed life altered the course of national events, events that would have killed and oppressed the masses.[3]

EVANGELISM ALWAYS HAS SOCIAL IMPLICATIONS

This certainly was one of the most bizarre encounters in my ministry, but one of only scores I know of in which evangelism proved the best form of social action.

In Leningrad shortly before the breakup of the former Soviet Union, a Russian reporter challenged me to give him one example demonstrating how the Gospel can change lives and society at large. I said gladly, and I told him about Rosario Rivera, one of the revolutionary Che Guevara's closest co-workers.

Rosario was a Peruvian Marxist who experienced one of the saddest childhoods I've ever heard of. Later she slipped into immorality, turned to violence, and became bitter toward God. After Guevara's death Rosario went to Lima, Peru's capital, where I happened to be preaching. She came to the stadium angry enough to kill me, but the Lord touched her heart. Early the next morning she trusted Jesus Christ and experienced a complete transformation.

Instead of resorting to violence to bring about social change, Rosario began to give bread and milk to the poor and provided practical help to hundreds of families living in the slums of that huge city. Countless thousands have benefitted from her ministry, and scores have found new life in Jesus Christ.[4]

A missionary couple who serve in The Netherlands told me about their co-worker, a former prostitute who grew up in Uruguay, South America. Several years ago, this woman attended an evangelistic rally where pop star Cliff Richard was singing and I was preaching. She was soundly converted and now is sharing the love of God in Holland's red-light districts. The change in her life has been dramatic, and the social implications widespread.

To suggest that evangelism makes no contribution to solving the world's problems ignores history. Slavery was abolished in Britain by a group of men who were converted to Christ in the evangelistic campaigns of John and Charles Wesley and George Whitefield. Justice and freedom under the law are a direct fruit of the Gospel. In South Africa Billy Graham's racially integrated crusade meetings in 1973 brought whites and blacks together in large public meetings for the first time in that country's history.

Evangelism always has social implications, because it takes place in a social context. In the first century, the Gospel bridged cultural barriers between man and woman, Jew and Gentile, slave and free. Paul called Onesimus, Philemon's slave, "our faithful and dear brother" (Colossians 4:9). Writing to Philemon, Paul said, "He is very dear to me but even dearer to you, both as a man and as a brother in the Lord" (Philemon 16).

The Gospel also confronted pagan customs and immoral practices. The Thessalonians "turned to God from idols" (1 Thessalonians 1:9). Fearing for their livelihood, silversmiths in Ephesus incited a riot. The Gospel as preached by Paul had robbed fertility goddess Artemis of worshipers and threatened to deprive idol-making silversmiths of unjust and exploitive profits (Acts 19).

When Zacchaeus met Jesus, the corrupt tax collector's dominating desire turned to charitable giving to the poor and restitution for those he had cheated (Luke 19).

Evangelism is the deepest and most profound social action in the world because it deals with the root of the problem, not with the symptoms alone. The root is man's alienation and sinfulness and evil. Most of the world's six billion people have yet to receive the Lord Jesus Christ as Savior. Their foremost need is the light of the Gospel—first to dispel spiritual darkness, but second to eradicate their utter selfishness.

The majority of people live for themselves; true Christians live for God and for others out of love. This love is implanted within all who put their faith and trust in Jesus Christ (1 John 3:16–4:21).

Tolstoy described his experience with Christ this way: "For thirty-five years of my life I was . . . a nihilist—not a revolutionary socialist, but a man who believed in nothing. Five years ago faith came to me . . . and my whole life underwent a sudden transformation. What I had once wished for I wished for no longer, and I began to desire what I had never desired before."

Imagine a city where tens of thousands of people experience the new birth and become new creations, like Zacchaeus. The Gospel can change society because it changes individuals, who then begin to change their families, which then change neighborhoods. And as those individuals live out their faith at home, in schools, in the military, in business, and in government, a quiet revolution occurs.

Most societies change by coercion. The few that change

by internal compulsion—without machine guns—are those that have had spiritual revivals.

Early eighteenth-century England was on the brink of disaster. Slave trade was at its highest. The barbarous prison system entertained the public with outdoor hangings. Gambling was a national obsession—one historian said England was a vast casino. False rumors manipulated the financial markets. The nation was almost drowned in liquor. "Every sixth house in London was a public house. Signs invited the poor to get drunk for a penny, dead-drunk for two-pence, and have straw on which to lie and recover free. Drunkenness was a national vice."[5]

Likewise, the national church and its pulpit were in decay. The dying church lost its power as moral and spiritual lethargy enveloped Britain. Instead of condemning the rampant sins of the era, ministers in empty churches read colorless essays void of true Christianity. Zeal for Christ was considered highly dangerous.

Bishop George Berkeley wrote in 1738 in his *Discourse Addressed to Magistrates and Men in Authority*, "The youth born and brought up in wicked times without any bias to good from early principle, or instilled opinion, when they grow ripe, must be monsters indeed. And it is to be feared that the age of monsters is not far off."[6]

But along came the Wesleys, George Whitefield, and the young men at Oxford known as the Holy Club. They fashioned what today we call a missions statement: "We want to reform the nation, particularly the church, and to spread scriptural holiness over the land." The Wesleyan revival, in turn, roused concern for public health, prison reform, and public education, perhaps sparing England the kind of revolution that bloodied France.

I am proud to preach the Gospel, the power of God,

because I cannot imagine anything that helps people more than introducing them to Jesus Christ. Evangelism saves people not only from dying without Christ, but also from living without Him. And as they live with Him and for Him, they become salt and light in a world lost in darkness, sorrow, conflict, violence, and fear.

It's the Gospel and its essential partner, prayer, that will change America. First-century Christians lived in a culture of terrible social evil. Infanticide, a horror equal to or even worse than abortion, was practiced throughout the Roman Empire. That was the world in which the Gospel came, and for the Apostle Paul that Gospel—"that Christ died for our sins according to the Scriptures, that he was buried, that he was raised on the third day according to the Scriptures" (1 Corinthians 15:3-4)—was *the* message. Proclamation of the Gospel was his primary course of action to confront and change a pagan society.

When anything but the Gospel becomes the church's top priority in its outreach to the world, we're merely feeding a corpse. Only the Gospel gives new life. Only the Gospel can change America.

TO PONDER

1. Read 2 Corinthians 5:17 again. How old were you when you committed your life to Jesus Christ? What was your life like before your conversion? What was it like afterward? What might your life be like today if you hadn't come to Christ?

2. "The people of this world create the problems of this world. If we can lead them to Christ, we will create a climate for other positive, practical changes to take place." What problems does the Gospel address head-on?

3. "Evangelism is the deepest, most profound, and most important social action in the world. It gives us hope in otherwise hopeless situations because God is stepping into hearts and lives. And what a difference that makes!" What is the most profound conversion you've witnessed? That you've heard about?

4. "To suggest that evangelism makes no contribution to solving the world's problems ignores history." How might the future of this country be different if we make evangelism our number one priority?

5. "Most societies change by coercion. The few that change by internal compulsion—without machine guns— are those that have had spiritual revivals." How do you suppose America's history might have been different if it weren't for the great revivals that have taken place about once every generation for the past 250 years?

6. "It's the Gospel and its essential partner, prayer, that will change America." Why is prayer so important? What does Scripture instruct us to pray about?

7. "When anything but the Gospel becomes the church's top priority in its outreach to the world, we're merely feeding a corpse. Only the Gospel gives new life. Only the Gospel can change America." What would you say are some of the church's priorities today? What will it take to make evangelism its first priority?

3

A MESSAGE
FOR AMERICA

For God so loved the world that he gave his
one and only Son, that whoever believes
in him shall not perish but have eternal life.
For God did not send his Son into the world
to condemn the world, but to save the
world through him. Whoever believes in him
is not condemned, but whoever does not
believe stands condemned already because
he has not believed in the name of God's one
and only Son.

— John 3:16-18

3

IN 1960 I WAS ON MY WAY TO AMERICA for graduate studies. At the airport in Buenos Aires for the first flight of my life, my mother just couldn't get enough advice into the few minutes we had left. As I was pulling away from her in my one and only brand-new black suit, she said, "Don't go into the cities, don't travel alone, watch out, don't get shot and stuffed in a trunk, and remember Hebrews 13:5 and 6!"

I confess to ignoring at least some of Mom's admonition. I love America's cities and couldn't wait for the day when I would preach the Gospel to tens of thousands in the nation's stadiums. Was that presumptuous for a young Argentine who hadn't yet preached to crowds much larger than a hundred in Latin America? I'll leave it to the Lord to judge my motives. I simply believe He gave me a special concern for this greatest of nations that would become my home.

For twenty-nine years, however, I clearly felt the restraint of the Holy Spirit. Until Billy Graham's crusade ministry slowed down in the United States, I believe God was leading our team to concentrate our crusades in Latin America, Europe, and Asia.

In 1989, however, the time had come for a new wave of national evangelization. My first thought was to ask for Billy Graham's blessing. "You don't need it, but if you want it, you've got it," Billy said to me. "We've got to get on with evangelism."

AMERICA IS AT A CROSSROADS

I love America. I became an American citizen in 1962. When I pledged allegiance at a ceremony in San Francisco, I put my hand over my heart, and today when the national anthem is sung, I'm one of the few in a crowd who still does that. President John Kennedy and Attorney General Robert Kennedy signed my citizenship document. I pull it out and look at it every Christmas. I frequently say to people who were born here, "You are an American by biological accident. I *chose* to become an American."

But something has gone wrong in our nation. America isn't the same country it was when I first arrived. In my opinion, everything began to change during the Vietnam War. Near the end of the war, I remember saying to my wife, "It seems like the demons of hell have invaded the United States."

Today, by George Barna's estimation based on large-scale surveys of the population, 190 million people in America have yet to accept Jesus Christ as their Savior. "The non-Christian segment of the national population is so extensive that if it were a nation, it would constitute the fifth most populated nation on planet earth."[1] As it is, the United States is the fourth largest mission field in the world.

America is at a crossroads. We've been in trouble

before, but just as the nation seemed destined for destruction, revival reversed the tide of corruption and moral decay. John and Charles Wesley, George Whitefield, Charles Finney, D. L. Moody, Billy Sunday, and the tireless Billy Graham—their gospel proclamation turned millions to Jesus Christ. Throughout this next decade and beyond, my team and I are committed to helping give America the same opportunity to hear the Good News at another critical hour in its history.

Los Angeles police detective Mark Fuhrman's expletive-laced tapes—disclosed during the O. J. Simpson murder trial—were an abhorrent reminder of racist evil in America that decades of effort have not expunged. Temple University criminologist James Fyfe, who has testified in police brutality cases, succinctly explained why: "It's difficult to change what's in an officer's heart."

America has a heart disorder that only the Gospel can fix. The Gospel gets at the root of the problems, not just the outward behavior.

Despondency

A spirit of despondency lies over the nation. We've lost hope. We need a positive message of God's love for the country, of what Christ can do for broken families, for the lonely, the addicted, the dying.

Those of us who stand in America's pulpits have to be careful not to dwell on the negative, to recite the headlines and review the talk shows. Disgusting stories that illustrate the authority of Satan or the influence of the world get people's attention, but before you know it, we're all sitting there paralyzed, forgetting the tremendous power of God.

The Gospel—"the power of God for the salvation of

everyone who believes" (Romans 1:16)—rejuvenates. Because of our freedom, America has always been a symbol of happy people, but freedom comes from the Gospel of Jesus Christ, who sets us free from slavery to sin. "If the Son sets you free, you will be free indeed" (John 8:36).

Divisiveness

A spirit of separatism divides America. It seems that everyone's a hyphenated American. My passport doesn't say Hispanic-American; it says citizen of the United States of America. Please don't make a point of calling attention to my ethnic heritage unless you're certain you know what it means.[2] During the O. J. Simpson trial, with the darkness of racism once again on public display before the world, one former Los Angeles police detective observed, "Instead of being multicultural and diverse, we should all just be Americans."

There's also generational confrontation. Young people are saying to retirees, "Give us back some of your Social Security money," not understanding how they fought in World War II, worked hard, saved money, and did their best.

Divided families contribute to generational confrontation. Divorce skyrocketed in the generation after World War II. More and more children felt abandoned. These children, now middle-aged adults, feel no responsibility for their parents. "My old man walked out on me. Let him fend for himself."

The forces trying to divide America have also infiltrated the church, the only institution that truly can and should show unity because we are blended into one family in Jesus Christ. "For we were all baptized by one Spirit into one body— whether Jews or Greeks, slave or free—and we were all given the one Spirit to drink" (1 Corinthians 12:13).

But of all the countries in the world, the United States is one of the toughest to get Christians to work together to evangelize their communities and cities. It's an amazing thing, because Americans will come together to watch football games. They'll come together for rock concerts. They'll even come together for politics. Sure, they're not "of one mind." But at least they're together. Why can't we who are in Christ come together for evangelism? How good it is to confront the city with the claims of Jesus Christ . . . together! It's the Gospel of Jesus Christ that will teach this country to be truly "one nation under God." Jesus Christ brings reconciliation— a deep, sincere love for people regardless of culture, age, race, or educational privilege.

Impurity

America needs a restored spirit of holiness. We have lost our sense of shame, our sense of what is proper and honorable. "Nothing seems to embarrass us; nothing shocks us anymore," says Colin Powell in his autobiography. "Spend time switching channels on daytime television, and you will find a parade of talk shows serving up dysfunctional people whose morally vacant behavior offers the worst possible models for others."[3]

A few years ago during a national crusade in Jamaica, I turned on the television to one or two American channels. To be honest, I was ashamed to be an American when I saw the degenerate entertainment our nation is exporting to the world.

Josh McDowell, whose "Why Wait?" and "Right from Wrong" campaigns are helping teenagers build their lives on biblical principles, received a letter from a father who was devastated by what he had just discovered. His oldest daughter had dated a boy on the school football team, and early in the relationship she had sex with him. She repeated this behavior with another football player, then another, and before long had slept with the whole team. Her father wrote, "Josh, they were passing my little girl around as some sort of team girl."

It's not enough to rave against immorality. It's really a sorry thing when nine-year-old girls and boys are being told about condoms and "safe sex," but getting all worked up about it isn't going to change anything. Only when millions of Americans convert to Jesus Christ and then begin to walk in the power of the Holy Spirit will America change. Let's not point the finger at people, but point the way to Jesus Christ. The celebrity who split up from her husband "after much thought and consideration" just seven months after their marriage and seven weeks after the birth of their son needs the Gospel, not condemnation.

With proclamation of the Gospel, believers must walk in holiness. I love what John MacArthur says: "If you think sin is fun, you should try holiness." There is joy in walking with God. If millions of believers were to model holiness, the church could again have a positive influence as in decades past.

Guilt

What America needs most, however, is forgiveness, preceded by repentance. An enormous cloud of guilt hangs over our people. Yet God is ready to forgive. He will forgive people who have had abortions. He will forgive adulterers and fornicators. He will forgive murderers and rapists and embezzlers. He will forgive the self-righteous and hypocrites. He forgives all of us sinners the instant we believe Him with a repentant heart.

During our Tulsa crusade, a young man named Kevin who was struggling with homosexual temptation called our live television program. After Kevin opened his heart to Jesus Christ, I asked if he could come to one of the crusade meetings at the Convention Center.

"It's been on my heart to come every night," Kevin said. "It's just that I felt like I had to be free from this guilt. . . . I felt too dirty to come."

"Kevin, you are not too dirty for Jesus," I replied, hardly able to hold back tears.

The major theme of my evangelistic preaching in America is the offer of free forgiveness through the blood of Jesus Christ. It is the entrance of truth into the souls of the American people. Though they may not articulate it, they may cover it up, they may even argue against it, Americans feel guilty. Most were brought up with a sense of right and wrong, a sense that sin is sin. They know they've messed up.

At an evangelical convention, I met several people infected with HIV through engaging in homosexual acts. I asked one brother how he found peace with God and knew for sure his sins were forgiven. "When I understood the Cross," he said. That's what brings peace to the conscience—the Cross of Christ.

It isn't enough to say, "God loves you and so do I." It's true and it's beautiful, but it's not enough. It's not enough to say, "It's not your fault," and blame sinful behavior on society, on a person's parents or spouse, or on some chemical imbalance.

In America many people have talked themselves into thinking they can cover up their guilt, but in moments of quietness, their conscience begins to speak.

MARKED BY ANGER

It seems as if the whole tone of America is confrontation. Evangelicals are getting far too angry about far too many things, to the detriment of the Gospel.

Our culture is increasingly interested in the spiritual. Check out the *New York Times* best-seller list. Newspaper opinion columns. Gallup polls. Barna polls. But when people come to church looking for God, for spiritual reality, and perhaps even for the forgiveness of sins, they are quite apt to hear a terse and prolonged position statement on abortion, homosexuality, or the latest White House policy statement.

Instead of compassionate, biblical love—the heart of the Gospel—being our defining mark to an unbelieving world, as commanded by the Lord Jesus Christ, we American evangelicals are now known nationally (and internationally) by our anger. And anger does not draw people to the Savior. It repels them. Scripture, to the contrary, states, "Do you not know that God's kindness is meant to lead you to repentance?" (Romans 2:4 RSV).

That message—that God is a loving God who forgives sinners and offers everyone the chance to start over—has transformed millions of lives all across Latin America during the past twenty-five years. Evangelicals, some illiterate, have stood on street corners preaching John 3:16 and testifying of God's grace. Millions of Latins have said, "That's the Gospel? I want to know this God and live for Him."

But in the United States, we evangelicals have acquired a reputation as harsh, unloving, bitter people, condemning to hell pregnant young women at abortion clinics and homosexuals marching in Washington.

If we stand and proclaim John 3:16 in its purity and with all the vigor of the Holy Spirit, I'm convinced that hundreds of thousands, if not millions, of Americans will listen and trust Jesus Christ for salvation.

> *Have mercy on me, O God,*
> *according to your unfailing love;*
> *according to your great compassion*
> *blot out my transgressions.*
> *Wash away all my iniquity*
> *and cleanse me from my sin.*
> *For I know my transgressions,*
> *and my sin is always before me.*
> *Against you, you only, have I sinned*
> *and done what is evil in your sight,*
> *so that you are proved right when you speak*
> *and justified when you judge.*
> — *Psalm 51:1-4*

That's the kind of repentance the Lord loves.

Jesus specializes in taking away guilt. It is a great thing when people confess their sins and let God forgive on the basis of the Cross and the blood of Jesus Christ. That's the only path to peace with God and a cleansed conscience. God is satisfied, not by psychiatry, not by good gestures, not by sincere statements, but by the Cross of Jesus Christ.

My dream is this: that a massive wave of evangelization restores America's days of glory, those spiritual days when joy pervaded the land. America was once young in spirit, vibrant, and full of hope. It can be again.

TO PONDER

1. Read John 3:16-18 again. How great is God's love for the people of this world? How important is each person's

response to His Son? What is the definite hope of all those who are saved?

2. "Today, by George Barna's estimation based on large-scale surveys of the population, 190 million Americans have yet to accept Jesus Christ as their Savior. [In other words] the United States is the fourth largest mission field in the world." According to the Bible, what is the actual destiny of those 190 million people if they reject Christ to their dying day? In contrast, what is God's desire? What is your heart's response to the great need to re-evangelize this nation?

3. "America has a disorder that only the Gospel can fix. The Gospel gets at the root of the problems, not just the outward behavior." What is the root of America's problems? What are some of the negative outward behaviors it creates? What are some of the most common "solutions" to such problems? How well have such "solutions" worked over the past twenty-five years?

4. "A spirit of despondency lies over the nation." What kind of despondency have you observed? In your opinion, how prevalent are such feelings of hopelessness across the nation?

5. "A spirit of separatism divides America." Over what are Americans divided? Over what are American Christians separated? How does such divisiveness within the church affect our witness to a watching world?

6. "America needs a restored sense of holiness. We have lost our sense of shame, our sense of what is proper and honorable." What do you think has caused such a dramatic change in our standards of "right" and "wrong"? What are some of today's most vehemently hated social

"sins"? How does that list compare with the sins decried in Scripture?

7. "What America needs most, however, is forgiveness, preceded by repentance. An enormous cloud of guilt hangs over our people. Yet God is ready to forgive." About what kinds of sins do many Americans feel guilty? What kind of people is God ready to forgive?

8. "Instead of a compassionate, biblical love—the heart of the Gospel—being our defining mark to an unbelieving world, as commanded by the Lord Jesus Christ, we American evangelicals are now known nationally (and internationally) by our anger." About what are some Christians getting vehemently angry? How is such anger a detriment to the Gospel?

9. "If we stand and proclaim John 3:16 in its purity and with all the vigor of the Holy Spirit, I'm convinced hundreds of thousands, if not millions, of Americans will listen and trust Jesus Christ for salvation." What sorts of things currently hinder such a massive, clear-cut proclamation of the Gospel to this nation?

10. "My dream is this: that a massive wave of evangelization restores America's days of glory, those spiritual days when joy pervaded the land. America was once young in spirit, vibrant, and full of hope. It can be again." What will it take for America to experience such a revival of real Christianity?

4

THE GOSPEL OF
RECONCILIATION

---

*Then Peter began to speak: "I now realize how
true it is that God does not show favoritism but
accepts men from every nation who fear him
and do what is right. You know the message God
sent to the people of Israel, telling the good news
of peace through Jesus Christ, who is Lord of all.
You know what has happened throughout
Judea, beginning in Galilee after the baptism
that John preached—how God anointed Jesus of
Nazareth with the Holy Spirit and power, and
how he went around doing good and healing all
who were under the power of the devil, because
God was with him. We are witnesses of everything he did in the country of the Jews and in
Jerusalem. They killed him by hanging him on a*

tree, but God raised him from the dead on the third day and caused him to be seen. He was not seen by all the people, but by witnesses whom God had already chosen—by us who ate and drank with him after he rose from the dead. He commanded us to preach to the people and to testify that he is the one whom God appointed as judge of the living and the dead. All the prophets testify about him that everyone who believes in him receives forgiveness of sins through his name."

While Peter was still speaking these words, the Holy Spirit came on all who heard the message. The circumcised believers who had come with Peter were astonished that the gift of the Holy Spirit had been poured out even on the Gentiles. For they heard them speaking in tongues and praising God.

Then Peter said, "Can anyone keep these people from being baptized with water? They have received the Holy Spirit just as we have." So he ordered that they be baptized in the name of Jesus Christ.

— Acts 10:34-48

4

ERNIE HORN IS AN UNLIKELY HERO, perhaps the last person you'd expect to see leading the way in healing racial divisions in Fort Worth, Texas. And not just because his grandfather owned slaves in Kentucky. Ernie, owner of E. Horn Construction Inc., lives a very comfortable life. Why get involved in the messy ugliness of racism?

In his heart, Ernie understood reconciliation with God through the death of His Son. It took years, however, to come face to face with reconciliation as a practical concept that deals with human beings in downtown Fort Worth.

The story begins June 26, 1993. Police Detective Donald Manning and his date were enjoying a late-night walk around a lake in an east Fort Worth park. As they headed back to their car, four men confronted them, one holding a gun.

Manning had removed his nine millimeter service weapon and was holding it in his right hand, hidden behind his back.

He told his date to move to the side. When she did, the man with the gun fired and hit Manning in the left side.

"Donnie was shot with a Tech 9," Ernie says. "That's a machine gun that will blow a hole in you the size of a football."

Detective Manning, twenty-eight, died. Three days later police arrested several young men after one of them bragged to friends, "A dude we were trying to jack [rob] pulled a gun and we shot him."

Ernie says Manning was "a cops' cop, the Roger Staubach of police officers in Fort Worth—dedicated, talented, happy-go-lucky." As the contractor for a couple of neighborhood police stations, Ernie got to know him fairly well and had opportunities to talk to him about the Lord.

In any city, a policeman's murder is headline news. In Fort Worth, a city besieged by gangs and divided by race, Manning's murder made everything worse. White cop killed by a black gang banger.

"LOOK AT THEIR EYES"

The day of Manning's funeral, Ernie was having lunch with Gary Turner, coordinator of our team's upcoming evangelistic crusade in Fort Worth. Running out of time, Gary went with Ernie to the funeral chapel. They managed to squeeze inside.

Ernie describes these next experiences as "supernatural." During the funeral service, he says he felt an "expectation" that he tried to rationalize and dismiss in the emotion of those moments. "But the Lord really spoke to me and said, 'I'm going to reveal to you the beginning of a new thing.'"

Afterward Ernie and Gary rushed to Ernie's truck and drove to beat the crowd to the cemetery for the interment service. Ernie watched as the funeral procession of more than two thousand people, including about five hundred police officers, approached the grave site. Again the Lord spoke to him: "Look at their eyes."

"That frightened me, because I didn't have any understanding of what I was supposed to be doing," he says.

As the flag covering Manning's casket was folded and presented to Manning's mother, Ernie again heard, "Look at their eyes."

"I looked, and there were like five hundred John Waynes, 357 Magnums strapped to their sides. Every one of them had on sunglasses. I couldn't see their eyes. But as they started pulling their sunglasses off and wiping the tears, I saw the same hopelessness that you see on television in the eyes of starving people."

Days later, at the weekly prayer meeting for the crusade, Ernie says the Lord spoke again: "If I can't send My people to be part of the solution, who am I going to send?"

Ernie prayed, "Lord, show us how we can be part of the solution and how we can come together."

That summer he helped mobilize community and denominational leaders to get involved in the crusade scheduled for October. People of all races began to come together.

"In doing this, I was aware that a lot of people thought I was a missile out of control. By what authority did I keep showing up at different things, like the crime commission, and trying to get all these churches to come together? God had given me a vision and was opening all these doors."

DARKNESS IN HIS HEART

Ernie obeyed the Lord's leading, but inside he felt unworthy. Increasing interaction with minorities through his crusade and community involvement was exposing a dark side of his heart: racial prejudice.

It showed up most overtly at work. Ernie had just hired additional iron workers—all white—for a construction project. Every interview with a black man concluded the same way: "We'll get back with you later."

"If God was fixin' to do a new thing, I had to get out of His way and let Him do it," he says. "I needed to repent of the racism and prejudice and selfishness in my heart."

Ernie and crusade leaders in Fort Worth called a meeting of some thirty black pastors from the area where the young man who shot Manning had grown up. Ernie's idea was to enlist their support for a youth rally in an inner-city park—to get people to work together toward solutions and overcome the hopelessness that most were feeling in isolation.

Sitting in a circle face to face with mostly black people, Ernie fought back tears. "I was feeling real insecure and frightened about addressing these people and telling them the vision about what Palau's team was doing, what was fixin' to happen, about God doing a new thing.

"And then I realized it wasn't stage fright. I was under conviction. As I looked into the eyes of these black pastors, I confessed to them my prejudice and sin, and how in my business I had acted with partiality. I wasn't born a racist; I was taught to be a racist by the significant people in my life. So I repented. I asked them to forgive me.

"I was feeling pretty good then, but all of a sudden I had that same insecure feeling again, and I had to repent for the sins of my father's generation. That sure was God, because I don't think about things like that. And then my grandfather's generation. I didn't even know a lot of all that. My grandfather died when I was real young, and I knew only what my relatives told me. And then I looked, and every one of the pastors was weeping. I had asked them to forgive me, and they in turn asked me to forgive them."

With only a few days' notice, about four thousand young people—including rival gang members of the Bloods and Crips—showed up at a "reconciliation rally" at a southeast Fort Worth park. A few weeks later, the Greater Fort Worth Crusade brought black and white, rich and poor together to work at solving the city's problems from the inside out.

EQUAL AT THE ALTAR

"Unless we change the heart, we haven't changed anything," I said at the crusade's final rally. That evening a drug dealer responded to the gospel invitation, giving his life to Jesus Christ. That same moment, a few feet away, a prominent Fort Worth physician was making that same commitment.

The day before, the crusade's youth night crowd of nine thousand erupted in applause as three inner-city gang members were the first to make their way to the area in front of the platform to profess their newfound faith in Christ. Spearheaded by my friend Ernie Horn, volunteers had canvassed inner-city neighborhoods, inviting young people to the crusade. Arrangements were made for buses to bring more than five hundred young people to the Convention Center.

Months after the crusade, Fort Worth's churches and community leaders continued to work together to change their city. Pastors, businessmen, and the city's superintendent of schools cooperated to bring motivational speaker Joseph Jennings to Fort Worth. He spoke to more than thirty thousand kids in seventeen schools. At three evening rallies at Baptist, Presbyterian, and Roman Catholic churches, Jennings told sixty-seven hundred young people and parents how the Lord had rescued him from drug use and gang activity, and then he invited the kids to give their lives to Jesus Christ. More than four hundred made first-time decisions for the Lord.[1]

"DIFFERENCES DON'T MATTER"

The crusade's erasure of racial lines between churches released resources that have benefitted the entire body of Christ in Fort Worth. "Without the crusade, Ernie and I would have been running in different circles, but now we're running in the same circle," says Howard Caver, pastor of World Missionary Baptist Church in the inner city. Howard is one of the black pastors who heard Ernie's confession. He says the "crusade whirlwind" in the city "stirred up a lot of activity that got Christians looking beyond their four walls." For example, an ongoing pastors' prayer group has helped remove racial, denominational, and size barriers.

"When we come together, our differences don't matter," Howard says. "I forget I'm a pastor of a small church. No one's thinking, *Who are you? You pastor only fifty people.* We've created such strong bonds, that's not a consideration."

About a year after the crusade, World Missionary Baptist Church was trying to start a Christian school for neighborhood children to make sure they get a good education with biblical values and to prevent kids from joining gangs. "God always calls us to something we're too small to do," Howard says.

By the middle of August, the church was short twenty-one hundred dollars to pay for renovations to the building for the school. Howard told the congregation Sunday morning that they needed to pray. "God's going to perform a miracle, we know—He's always faithful—but we only have until tomorrow to get it done."

As he started his sermon, several men entered the church. They were Christian brothers Howard had met through prayer efforts for the crusade. About a hundred others from their congregation, James Avenue Baptist Church, followed them in. "We'd like to interrupt your service," one of the men said.

The surprise guests from James Avenue announced that their congregation's entire offering that morning was being given to their sister church for their school. They presented a check for nine thousand dollars, enough not only for building renovations, but now the teacher could be paid.

When Howard read the amount of the check, the roof was lifted with hallelujahs and amens, by both congregations.

"This would not have occurred without ministers coming together to pray and work," Howard says. "Whatever Christ asks you to do, it may be impossible for you alone, but remember, you've got the body [of Christ]. If we keep off to our little selves because we are Baptist or black or white or whatever, we're going to miss the other part of the body ministering to us because we've amputated our hand. That's what I'm telling people wherever I go. Open yourself up to the walls coming down. They shouldn't have been there in the first place."[2]

GOOD NEWS FOR ALL

As demonstrated in Fort Worth, Christ can bring reconciliation—a deep, sincere love for people regardless of culture, race, or educational privilege. The Gospel is good news for *all* men and women. "You are all sons of God through faith in Christ Jesus, for all of you who were baptized into Christ have clothed yourselves with Christ. There is neither Jew nor Greek, slave nor free, male nor female, for you are all one in Christ Jesus" (Galatians 3:26-28).

Jesus was the master of surprise, continually astonishing

people, especially by His choices of association. It's clear that
He orchestrated the encounter with the Samaritan woman
(John 4) not only to reveal Himself as the Messiah to an entire
village, but also to give His disciples a preview of their worldwide mission following His resurrection. What did the disciples
see when Jesus told them to "open your eyes and look at the
fields! They are ripe for harvest" (John 4:35)? Despised
Samaria. It was Samaritans who proclaimed Jesus "the Savior
of the world" (John 4:42).

Peter was with the Lord in Samaria for this object lesson,
and he was also present when the Lord commanded His followers to "go and make disciples of all nations" (Matthew
28:19) and "be my witnesses in Jerusalem, and in all Judea and
Samaria, and to the ends of the earth" (Acts 1:8). But he was a
slow learner, perhaps from cultural and ethnic prejudice. It
took a peculiar vision and the Holy Spirit's specific directions
to convince Peter to associate with a Gentile—the Roman centurion Cornelius—and preach the Gospel to him and his house-
hold (Acts 10).

Peter knew the Gospel was for all people. He acknowl-
edged its inclusiveness in his sermon: "All the prophets testify
about [Jesus] that everyone who believes in him receives forgiveness of sins through his name" (Acts 10:43). But prejudice
is a toxin difficult to clean up, as Christians in America know
all too well.

I've felt the hurt of prejudice. Fifteen months after I came
to America, my Anglo-Saxon bride, Patricia, and I were sent to
an intensive missionary training program in Detroit. One day
an elderly man, the pastor of the church where we were serving, approached my wife and in a confidential, "I'm-on-your-
side-dear" tone said to her, "You're probably going to suffer
great misunderstandings with your husband. If he ever mis-
treats you or beats you, let me know."

In his ignorance, this minister thought all Latins beat their wives, and he needed to protect her from me!

I'm used to prejudice. As Bible-believing Christians in Argentina, my parents endured hostility. Our family, though successful in business above most in town, was looked down upon. In school a teacher made me kneel on corn husks because of my evangelical beliefs. My mother and father counseled, encouraged, and motivated by teaching us, "In this world you will have trouble. But take heart! I have overcome the world" (John 16:33).

A number of years ago, a European minister—prominent around the world—said to me, "We hear good things about your ministry in South America, and we thank God for all that's happening there." Then he pointedly added, "I think you'd be better off just preaching to your people."

But later, when I preached the Gospel at a united citywide crusade in his country, this same minister sat on the platform. Today I seek his counsel. In many ways, both of us have grown in the grace of God's message of reconciliation.

TO PONDER

1. Read Acts 10:34-38 again. What does this pivotal passage teach about the gospel message?

2. "Unless we change the heart, we haven't changed anything." What does it take for reconciliation to begin?

3. "The erasure of racial lines between churches releases resources that benefit the entire body of Christ." What racial lines exist between churches in your city? How would the body of Christ in your city benefit if those lines were erased?

4. "Jesus Christ can bring reconciliation—a deep, sincere love for people regardless of culture, race, or educational privilege. The Gospel is good news for all men and women." What evidences of this have you seen or heard in your city? What evidences would you like to witness in the future?

5. "Jesus was the master of surprise, continually astonishing people, especially by His choices of association." What was He trying to teach His disciples? How long did it take for them to learn that vital lesson? What will it take for us to get it?

6. Read Acts 10, the entire chapter. What did it take for Peter to preach the Gospel for the first time to a non-Jewish person? Then read Acts 11:1-18. How did other Jewish believers respond when they first heard what Peter had done? When they heard the full account of what God had accomplished among the Gentiles?

7. "Prejudice is a toxin difficult to clean up." What are the sources of that toxin in America? How long has the toxin poisoned our nation? What is the solution to cleaning it up? How long might that take?

5

WHO'S TELLING THE GOSPEL TRUTH?

Now, brothers, I want to remind you of the
gospel I preached to you, which you received
and on which you have taken your stand.
By this gospel you are saved, if you hold firmly
to the word I preached to you. Otherwise, you
have believed in vain. For what I received
I passed on to you as of first importance:
that Christ died for our sins according to the
Scriptures, that he was buried, that he was
raised on the third day according to the
Scriptures, and that he appeared to Peter, and
then to the Twelve. After that, he appeared to
more than five hundred of the brothers at the
same time.

— 1 Corinthians 15:1-6

5

"WHY HIM?" MORE THAN A FEW PEOPLE asked that question during D. L. Moody's evangelistic campaigns throughout Great Britain during the 1870s. Thousands were coming to faith in Jesus Christ, and whole cities were beginning to sing the praises of God. The impact of the Gospel was astonishing.

Yet Moody himself was considered anything but extraordinary. His education was limited. His speech was unimpressive. His messages were short and simple. Nevertheless, everywhere Moody preached hundreds were publicly coming forward to confess the Lord Jesus as Savior.

In Birmingham, England, one theologian went so far as to tell Moody, "The work is most plainly from God, for I can see no relation between yourself and what you have done." Moody laughed and replied, "I should be very sorry if it were otherwise."

LESSONS FROM GREAT EVANGELISTS

Why Moody? Why Wesley, Calvin, Luther, Zwingli, Zinzendorf, Whitefield, Finney, Spurgeon, Torrey, John Sung, Billy Sunday, Corrie ten Boom, Catherine Booth, and Billy Graham? There have been thousands of evangelists during the closing centuries of this millennium. But only a few were truly great. What made them great evangelists?

I've examined that question and found that the answer has little to do with method or technique. Some preached before the masses, some in churches. Some presented the Gospel in small groups, some one on one. Most of the great evangelists used a combination of approaches. But that isn't what made them great.

No, it wasn't their method, but their message—and their passion for souls that constrained them to tell everyone about the Savior to their dying day. "I would sooner wear out than rust out," George Whitefield said. The Gospel—that Christ died for our sins, was buried, and was raised on the third day—was their mission.

I was in Glasgow, Scotland, for a crusade about twenty-five years after Billy Graham had preached there. The story was told of an old Church of Scotland minister who went to hear Billy Graham each evening. When the crusade was over, the minister said, "Dr. Graham, I've heard you every night for six weeks, and you've preached the same sermon every single night."

Except for the introduction and illustrations, that's been true throughout Billy Graham's ministry. The Gospel hasn't changed in nearly two thousand years!

METHODS AREN'T SACRED

Moody once observed, "A lie will travel around the world while truth is still putting on its boots." A scientist, Sir Francis Bacon, put it this way: "Man prefers to believe what he prefers to be true." Frequently, we unwittingly believe false statements because we don't bother to scrutinize what we hear or read.

Many popular misconceptions about science or history are relatively harmless. Misconceptions about the work of God, however, may have eternal consequences. Many Christians would agree with this statement: "While 'mass' evangelism methods seem to have more results, 'personal' evangelism methods win people to Christ more effectively." There's only one problem—it's not true.

The idea that God advocates one form of evangelism over another is a serious theological error. Evangelism methods aren't sacred. They are simply vehicles for proclaiming the Gospel of Jesus Christ to the unsaved.

In this age of misinformation when millions do not understand the Gospel and are going to hell, we have no time to waste arguing about which approach to evangelism is "best." God does the work of evangelism through us, no matter what method we use. It is through the power of the Holy Spirit and by God's grace—not our impressive techniques—that people are saved. Polished evangelism presentations are weak and ineffective without His anointing.

"I came to you in weakness and fear, and with much trembling," the Apostle Paul admitted to the Christians in Corinth. "My message and my preaching were not with wise and persuasive words, but with a demonstration of the Spirit's power, so that your faith might not rest on men's wisdom, but on God's power" (1 Corinthians 2:3-5).

In spite of Paul's "weakness," many committed their lives to Christ, and the church in Corinth was established. Why? Because Paul willingly and actively proclaimed the Gospel using every available method. Paul used a variety of methods to win people to Christ. He could say, "I have become all things to all men so that by all possible means I might save some" (1 Corinthians 9:22).

Those evangelists considered great all shared a holy audacity that prompted them to try new approaches. In God's name they even sanctified the media to communicate the Gospel of Jesus Christ. Somebody once asked me, "Do you think if Jesus were here He would be on television?" Of course. If Paul were here, would he have a press conference? Definitely. He would do anything to get the attention of the city. Any method is valid as long as it is ethical and moral. There are no biblical restraints on methodology, only on the message.

GREATNESS IN SIMPLICITY

When baseball legend Mickey Mantle was playing for the New York Yankees, he went all out, both at the ball park during a game and at the bar afterward. He derisively referred to his Christian teammate Bobby Richardson as "that milk drinker." After Mantle underwent a liver transplant in 1994, he telephoned Richardson and asked for his prayers. A few days before he died of cancer, Mantle told his former teammate that he had become a born-again Christian. Looking for assurance that "the Mick" indeed had eternal life, Richardson asked why God should let him into heaven. "For God so loved the world that He gave His only begotten Son," Mantle responded.

If you want to know the biblical Gospel, there it is. D. L. Moody, called "an apostle of the love of God," was known to preach night after night on this one verse of Scripture. The sermons of all the great evangelists were incredibly Christ-centered. They had come to town to talk about Jesus.

Thank God that Bobby Richardson and other Christians told Mickey Mantle about Jesus, but we can't take for granted that all Americans know the Gospel. In fact, George Barna says most do not. Seventy-five percent of American adults do not know what John 3:16 says, and 63 percent cannot define "the Gospel."[1]

"To suggest that we have done all that we can and have successfully reached every adult with the gospel message blurs the distinction between *exposure* to the Gospel and truly *hearing* the Gospel. Just as Jesus had to teach the same basic lesson to His closest associates again and again, we may have to proclaim the Gospel to the same people, time after time, in various contexts, with a variety of applications, before they truly absorb the implications and importance of what we are sharing."[2]

There's tremendous Bible teaching in America today, but both in the media and in general witness the pure Gospel of John 3:16 and 1 Corinthians 15:1-6 is not being proclaimed. Teaching about the family is good, but it's not the Gospel. Talking about politics is helpful, but it's not the Gospel. Calling for a return to values and virtues is admirable, but it's not the Gospel. We have to get back to the gospel basics.

STRAIGHT FROM THE HEART OF GOD

What is the Gospel? The Billy Graham Evangelistic Association invited me to speak on "Know the Biblical Message" at the Christian Workers' Conference, part of Global Mission, which went out by satellite to 185 countries. Here's what I said to half a million pastors and lay workers around the world:

The Gospel comes from the heart of God.

"God is love" (1 John 4:8). Americans must hear over and over again that God truly loves them. He wants everyone to be saved (1 Timothy 2:4). He wants everyone to come to repentance (2 Peter 3:9).

The Gospel is based on the shed blood of Jesus Christ on the cross.

Jesus Christ died for our sins. Many people ask, "Don't all religions lead to God?" No. Many religions don't even make that promise. Jesus said, "I am the way and the truth and the life. No one comes to the Father except through me" (John 14:6). Why could He be so exclusive? Because He's the only one who died on a cross for the sins of the world—for your sins and mine. He died in our place. A minister once asked Charles Spurgeon if he could put into a few words his Christian faith. "It is all in four words," Spurgeon replied. "Jesus died for me!"

Jesus Christ was buried. His burial is proof that He truly died, and all our sins were buried with Him. "We were therefore buried with him through baptism into death in order that, just as Christ was raised from the dead through the glory of the Father, we too may live a new life" (Romans 6:4). Praise God, we don't have to carry a load of guilt on our conscience.

Jesus Christ was raised on the third day. He is alive today! There is no tomb holding His bones. We don't build monuments to Christ because He's not dead.

Jesus Christ ascended into heaven. Just as He went up, the Bible says, He will come again and take us to Himself. "Do not let your hearts be troubled. Trust in God; trust also in me. In my Father's house are many rooms; if it were not so, I would have told you. I am going there to prepare a place for you. And if I go and prepare a place for you, I will come back and take you to be with me that you also may be where I am" (John 14:1-3).

The Gospel is a call from God to repent and believe in the Lord Jesus Christ.

Without an invitation to repent and believe (Acts 2:38;

3:19; 16:31; 17:30), the Gospel is incomplete. To believe in Jesus is to receive Him (John 1:12), to open the door (Revelation 3:20), to confess Him (Romans 10:9-10), which means we are not ashamed of Jesus.

God calls every single individual to Himself. "In the past God overlooked such ignorance, but now he commands all people everywhere to repent" (Acts 17:30). He *commands* repentance; it isn't a suggestion.

Repentance is one side of the coin. The other side is to believe. "Believe in the Lord Jesus, and you will be saved" (Acts 16:31). The testimony of the Thessalonian Christians had become known everywhere. "They tell how you turned to God from idols to serve the living and true God, and to wait for his Son from heaven, whom he raised from the dead" (1 Thessalonians 1:9-10). Their lives demonstrated true repentance and belief.

That's the Gospel, pure and simple. The older I get, the bolder I become to stick with the basics, to proclaim the Gospel with simplicity. Its power is amazing.

CONVERSION WITHOUT THERAPY

We've got to believe in instantaneous conversions again, what Moody called "instant salvation." Calvin wrote in his commentary on the Psalms, " . . . by sudden conversion, [God] subdued and made teachable a heart which, for my age, was far too hardened." I love that phrase, "by sudden conversion." I believe in recent decades the United States and Western Europe have not seen as many conversions to Christ as many countries in Asia and Latin America because we're not sure if Christ has the power to convert people on the spot. The "gospel" that many preach says, "If you believe in the Lord Jesus Christ, get into a therapy group, and hang in there a few years, you never know—one of these days He just might liberate you from addiction." That's an anemic gospel whose fruit is wimpy conversions, "a different gospel—which is really no gospel at all" (Galatians 1:6-7).

The Gospel preached by the Apostle Paul came "with power, with the Holy Spirit and with deep conviction" (1 Thessalonians 1:5). That Gospel says, "Christ can set you free—now!" If we proclaim the biblical Gospel, I believe that thousands of Americans will be changed overnight. The living Christ has the power to do it.

TO PONDER

1. Read 1 Corinthians 15:1-6 again. According to this key passage of Scripture, what is the essential gospel message? How widely is that message known in America? How widely is it believed?

2. "There have been thousands of evangelists during the closing centuries of this millennium. But only a few were truly great." Who were some of these great evangelists? What made them great evangelists?

3. "The Gospel hasn't changed in nearly two thousand years." What are some common American misconceptions about what makes someone a real Christian?

4. "The idea that God advocates one form of evangelism over another is a serious theological error. Evangelism methods aren't sacred. They are simply vehicles for proclaiming the Gospel of Jesus Christ to the unsaved." Which methods have you used to help proclaim the Gospel to others? Which methods would you like to try?

5. "The sermons of all the great evangelists were incredibly Christ-centered. They had come to town to talk about Jesus." Do you think such evangelists might have ever tired of preaching the same message over and over? Why or why not?

6. "Seventy-five percent of Americans do not know what John 3:16 says, and 63 percent cannot define 'the Gospel.'" What do those statistics suggest about the way we present the Gospel to unbelievers? What can we assume they already understand?

7. "There's tremendous Bible teaching in America today, but both in the media and in general witness the pure Gospel of John 3:16 and 1 Corinthians 15:1-6 is not being proclaimed. Teaching about the family is good, but it's not the Gospel. Talking about politics is helpful, but it's not the Gospel. Calling for a return to values and virtues is admirable, but it's not the Gospel. We have to get back to the basics." What are the gospel basics?

8. "The older I get, the bolder I become to stick with the basics, to proclaim the Gospel with simplicity. Its power is amazing." According to Romans 1:16, why should we be proud of the power of the Gospel?

9. "I believe in recent decades the United States and Western Europe have not seen as many conversions to Christ as many countries in Asia and Latin America because we're not sure if Christ has the power to convert people on the spot." Why are some unsure of the Gospel's power? What has taken the place of the church's belief in sudden conversion?

10. "If we proclaim the biblical Gospel, I believe that thousands of Americans will be changed overnight. The

living Christ has the power to do it." What does Scripture teach about conversion? Is someone always changed instantaneously? In every area of life? If not, which areas?

_6_

GOOD WORKS AREN'T GOOD ENOUGH

For it is by grace you have been saved, through faith—and this not from yourselves, it is the gift of God—not by works, so that no one can boast.

— Ephesians 2:8-9

6

WILLY WAS A MINISTER with seventeen years in the pastorate and two theological degrees, and now he was helping with preparations for a huge crusade in his city. I had just finished teaching on 2 Corinthians at a pre-crusade leadership retreat, and as we headed to lunch in the dining room Willy said, "You know, Luis, these Bible studies are really exciting. You seem to believe every word of Scripture."

"Willy, I do," I said. "Don't you?"

"In my seminary we just figured the basic ideas were inspired, but not the words," he said.

Statements like that questioning the authority of Scripture always start the bells ringing and flags waving in my mind, and I thought, *I wonder if Willy knows the Lord?*

"Willy, do you have eternal life?" I asked.

Willy seemed to welcome the question. "About a month ago two of your team members stayed at my house, and they were telling their testimonies," he said. "They seemed so excited about eternal life. When I went to bed, I said to my wife, 'Dear, do you have eternal life?' And she said, 'Willy, you know I don't. Do you?'" The couple talked until five in the morning.

Willy was ready for the Gospel, and before we finished lunch, he opened his heart to Jesus Christ. Four months later, on the closing day of the crusade, Willy's wife and three children came to Christ. They all walked forward and hugged each other in front of the whole crowd.

In another crusade city, as I counseled people who called our television program in search of spiritual help and prayed on the air with those who wanted to receive Christ, the station manager standing in the studio listened intently.

"I don't understand it," he said to me as the program signed off. "I attend church every Sunday. I partake of holy Communion. I do confession at the stated times. And yet I have no assurance of eternal life."

Unfortunately, millions of Americans share the station manager's uncertainty and Willy's long quest, because they are trusting their own efforts—especially religious observances—to get them into paradise. This kind of thinking permeates all religions, including traditional Christianity.

From the moment Adam disobeyed God in the garden, man has sought his own way to cover his sin and cleanse his conscience. We desire *to do*. We ask the same question the crowd asked Jesus: "What must we do to do the works God requires?" (John 6:28).

And God has always replied, "There's nothing you can do. You must trust Me to do it for you." Jesus answered the crowd, "The work of God is this: to believe in the one he has sent" (John 6:29).

WHY DO WE THINK
WRONGLY?

Pride can be at the center of this conflict—we like to think we're self-sufficient. But in our biblically illiterate culture, ignorance is often to blame. If 75 percent of American adults do not know what John 3:16 says, one can only imagine how Ephesians 2:8-9, probably the best-known text on faith and works, would score in a poll.

Righteousness through faith, not works, excludes boasting, Paul writes in Romans 3:21-31. Even the extraordinary works of Abraham, "the father of us all" (Romans 4:16), were impotent to win God's acceptance.

"If, in fact, Abraham was justified by works, he had something to boast about—but not before God. What does the Scripture say? 'Abraham believed God, and it was credited to him as righteousness'" (Romans 4:2-3).

The parable of the Pharisee (a strict religious legalist) and the tax collector (whom Jews considered a cheating traitor) presents the same contrast. "Two men went up to the temple to pray," Jesus said. "The Pharisee stood up and prayed about himself: 'God, I thank you that I am not like other men—robbers, evildoers, adulterers—or even like this tax collector. I fast twice a week and give a tenth of all I get.'

"But the tax collector stood at a distance. He would not even look up to heaven, but beat his breast and said, 'God, have mercy on me, a sinner.'

"I tell you that this man, rather than the other, went home justified before God. For everyone who exalts himself will be humbled, and he who humbles himself will be exalted" (Luke 18:10-14).

THE FINISHED WORK OF CHRIST

Good works aren't good enough to earn God's acceptance, to find peace with God, to pay the debt for sin. No matter how hard we try and how sincere our efforts, our consciences will never be cleansed "from acts that lead to death" (Hebrews 9:14). Instead we must come to God on His terms—not by our works but by trust in the finished work of His Son.

God's work of salvation in Jesus Christ was finished nearly two thousand years before I was born, long before I committed my first sin, let alone before I repented and believed. It is finished, and there's nothing I can add.

When we think that good behavior somehow contributes to our salvation, we commit two grievous wrongs:

First, we diminish the death of Jesus Christ. Dare we imply that this provision for our sin, planned by our wise, all-knowing, and all-powerful God, wasn't enough for redemption? If this is true, why did God the Son endure the shame and horror of the cross?

Second, we deny man's helpless condition. The Bible says we were "dead in transgressions" before God "made us alive with Christ" (Ephesians 2:5). We followed the ways of this world, "gratifying the cravings of our sinful nature and following its desires and thoughts" (Ephesians 2:2-3). We are incapable of paying even one-hundredth of one percent of our debt to God. "A man get to heaven by works!" Whitefield said in his last sermon. "I would as soon think of climbing up to the moon on a rope of sand!"

Herein is the danger of religion. There is good in every religion, but only one Savior who died for our sins. Every religion gives good advice. But good advice is based on the premise that human beings have the ability to carry it out and that this success will somehow cleanse our guilty conscience.

Good works, even *religious* observance, contribute nothing to our salvation. "But when the kindness and love of God our Savior appeared, he saved us, not because of righteous things we had done, but because of his mercy" (Titus 3:4-5).

During a nationwide call-in television program, I talked to a young woman named Joanie who told me that, although she was about to be baptized at her church, she carried a lot of guilt from her past. She had no confidence that God heard her prayers. Joanie had religion but not a relationship with Jesus Christ. She had never placed her faith in Him as her Savior.

Bryan Houston, the news anchor at KETK-TV in Tyler, Texas, was baptized twice—and yet "I just didn't get it," he told a crowd during the Greater East Texas Crusade in 1995. His first baptism was at age eleven, on the same day he was confirmed. "I thought that was what you're supposed to do," he said. "I knew about Jesus Christ, that He died on the cross for my sins, but it was like a fact I might learn in any class at school." Bryan was baptized again at age thirty-one, this time by immersion, because the church he wanted to join required it.

Some months later, Bryan attended a conference where the preacher gave a gospel invitation and asked, "Are you really, really sure that if you died right now, at this very instant, you would go to heaven?" Bryan wasn't sure. "All my life all I've been doing is joining churches," he said. "But that night I asked Jesus Christ to come into my heart. Since that time, the one thing I absolutely know without question, in the darkest of times and when things are going great, is that when I do die, I am going to be with my Father in heaven."

Joanie and Bryan were like millions of Americans. In nationwide surveys, Barna Research Group has discovered that half of all adults who attend Protestant churches on a typical Sunday morning are not genuine Christians. They live "without having a shred of insight" into what a relationship with Christ is all about.[1]

Barna encourages Christians not to take for granted that their friends and acquaintances at church have truly committed their lives to Christ. "Do they acknowledge His earthly existence, His death and resurrection, His heavenly presence today, His ability to forgive sins, and His unique standing as the One who will determine our eternal fate? Yes. Have they complied with the biblical mandate to ask for His forgiveness for their sins and to acknowledge that He, and He alone, is able to dismiss our failings and gain us entry into God's presence for eternity? Well, in their minds, yes, as evidenced by their church attendance, by their donations to ministry activity, and by their acknowledgment of His deity and supremacy."[2]

Church attendance. Tithing. Baptism. Communion. These are signs and symbols of salvation, but not—most definitely not—salvation itself.

LET'S NOT KNOCK GOOD WORKS

It's not that God dislikes good works, however. In fact, He commends them. He didn't knock the prayers and generous giving of Cornelius the centurion, described in Scripture as devout and God-fearing. "Your prayers and gifts to the poor have come up as a memorial offering before God," an angel said to him (Acts 10:4).

I used to think I had to confront people who believed their good works would get them to heaven. Now I start off positively. "Your good works show you have a proper fear of God. I'm sure He is glad that you're trying to please Him," I might say. "But you must come to know God the way He has devised."

Good works can go in two directions. They can reveal a sincere, broken desire to know God by pleasing Him. Or they can reveal an unrepentant desire to pacify God, covering up rather than exposing sin.

In my experience, most people who rely on good works are at least admitting that they have a problem with God. Good works are their sincere, though unenlightened, effort to solve it (Romans 10:2-3). When they hear and understand the revealed Gospel, many trust Christ immediately.

It is after conversion that we are to "spur one another on toward love and good deeds" (Hebrews 10:24). Good works are the *outcome* of faith. Good works are a logical, loving response to the mercy and grace of God, and a fruit of the Holy Spirit who has now come to live within us. "For we are God's workmanship, created in Christ Jesus to do good works, which God prepared in advance for us to do" (Ephesians 2:10).

True saving faith inevitably leads to good works—doing the revealed will of God. Obedience is faith in action.

"But someone will say, 'You have faith; I have deeds.' Show me your faith without deeds, and I will show you my faith by what I do" (James 2:18-19). Good works reveal our faith. "As the body without the spirit is dead, so faith without deeds is dead" (James 2:26). We work for God and for good because we are saved, not seeking to be saved.

A good deed in the eyes of God is not something we choose to do. Good works are obedience to God's revealed commands. An honest Christian will always feel that his good works are certainly less than perfect. But he's at peace with imperfection because he's not basing his right standing with God on his good deeds. Daily he proclaims, "My soul will boast in the Lord"—alone (Psalm 34:2). That's what salvation is all about.

TO PONDER

1. Read Ephesians 2:8-9. How are we saved? Why don't our works have anything to do with salvation?

2. "Millions of Americans are trusting their own efforts—especially religious observance—to get them into paradise. This kind of thinking permeates all religions, including traditional Christianity." Why do many people seem bent on *doing* good works to—at least partially—earn their salvation? What are some of the causes of such wrong thinking?

3. "When we think that good behavior somehow contributes to our salvation, we commit two grievous wrongs." What are those wrongs?

4. "Herein is the danger of religion. There is good in every religion but only one Savior who died for our sins." If every religion has some good, should we really consider non-Christian religions dangerous? Why or why not?

5. "In nationwide surveys, Barna Research Group has discovered that half of all Americans who attend Protestant churches on a typical Sunday morning are not genuine Christians. They live 'without having a shred of insight' into what a relationship with Christ is all about." Do they believe the basic facts about Jesus Christ? Yes. Do they think they're Christians? Yes. What's the problem?

6. "Good works can go in two directions. They can reveal a sincere, broken desire to know God by pleasing Him. Or they can reveal an unrepentant desire to pacify God, covering up rather than exposing sin." Whom do you know who is sincerely trying to please God by his or her good works? When the opportunity arises, what might

you say to this person to encourage him or her to trust Christ for salvation?

7. "In my experience, most people who rely on good works are at least admitting that they have a problem with God. Good works are their sincere, though unenlightened, effort to solve it (Romans 10:2-3). When they hear and understand the revealed Gospel, many trust Christ immediately." Whom do you know who is religious but not a real Christian yet? What can you do to remind yourself daily to pray by name for that person's salvation?

7

THE FUTURE OF
CRUSADE EVANGELISM

---

*Then Peter stood up with the Eleven, raised his
voice and addressed the crowd: "Fellow Jews and
all of you who live in Jerusalem, let me explain
this to you; listen carefully to what I say. . . .
Therefore let all Israel be assured of this:
God has made this Jesus, whom you crucified,
both Lord and Christ."*

*When the people heard this, they were cut to the
heart and said to Peter and the other apostles,
"Brothers, what shall we do?"*

*Peter replied, "Repent and be baptized, every one
of you, in the name of Jesus Christ for the
forgiveness of your sins. And you will receive the
gift of the Holy Spirit. The promise is for you and*

your children and for all who are far off—

for all whom the Lord our God will call."

With many other words he warned them; and

he pleaded with them, "Save yourselves

from this corrupt generation." Those who

accepted his message were baptized, and about

three thousand were added to their number

that day.

— Acts 2:14, 36-41

7

AS LONG AS THE LORD CONTINUES to instill in certain believers a passion for souls, there is a great future for crusade evangelism. Think of such choice servants of God as John Wesley, George Whitefield, D. L. Moody, and Billy Graham. They practiced "mass" evangelism[1] and their lives have touched millions. Each one's influence continues even today. And by the grace of God, servants like them will be raised up in the future!

"Some analysts have said stadium crusades would fall out of favor in the United States before the end of the century," says former *Los Angeles Times* religion writer Russell Chandler. "Not so. In fact, crowds in five—even six—figures will be packing the arenas, domes, and bleachers for the foreseeable future. Televised, video-taped, and satellite-remote events will reach millions, but they won't eliminate the need for the big-scale evangelistic meetings."[2]

C. Peter Wagner, professor of church growth at Fuller

Theological Seminary, says, "I believe that the best days of city-wide crusade evangelism are yet ahead."[3]

Just as in the days of most of the revivals recorded in history, mass evangelism remains and will remain one of the most powerful tools that God has placed in our hands—particularly in this generation. Why? Because today crusade evangelism means not only huge gatherings of people in stadiums and arenas, but also the use of radio, television, and all the other modern media to communicate the Gospel.

I emphatically believe in the future of crusade evangelism for the following reasons:

1. *Through united, citywide crusades, mass evangelism communicates God's truth to multiplied thousands of people.*

Our objective is to please God, and the New Testament clearly states that proclaiming God's truth is His deepest desire for us, even if our listeners refuse to hear or believe (Matthew 28:18-20; Mark 13:10; Luke 24:46-48).

God is pleased when we proclaim His Gospel before the masses, and that's exactly what the apostles did all the way through the book of Acts. Why? Because while one-on-one evangelism is crucial, it's impossible to win the world to Jesus Christ one person at a time. People are born into this world and die faster than we can reach them unless we take advantage of a multiplicity of methods to reach the masses.

Why is mass evangelism essential? An evangelist preaching the Gospel to an average of six thousand people per day for seventy days out of the year (a very realistic pace) will reach more than ten million people in less than twenty-five years. Another evangelist presenting the Gospel one on one to fifteen persons per day 365 days a year (a humanly impossible rate) would need nearly two thousand years to reach as many people for Jesus Christ.[4]

2. *Through crusade evangelism, entire cities and often nations become God-conscious.*

An awareness of the Gospel sweeps through the people. A sense of interest and expectancy touches the conscience of thousands. People start asking questions about life after death; victory over selfishness, temptation, and guilt; happiness and harmony in the home; honesty and justice in all aspects of life. Conversations in restaurants, offices, and homes focus on God and the Bible.

This God-consciousness provoked by citywide crusades thus becomes an amazing bridge to the souls of men. Believers suddenly find abundant opportunities to witness, and they do so with authority. At a civic function in Tyler, Texas, during the Greater East Texas Crusade in September 1995, Jesus Christ was as much a part of the conversation as high school football and the Dallas Cowboys—in the football-crazy Lone Star State! "It's easy to talk about Jesus in town this week," one man told me.

3. *Crusade evangelism arrests the attention of government leaders and other people of great influence.*

Well-attended crusades shake up the powers that be, because politicians and other national leaders understand a crowd. It causes them to listen to something they otherwise would ignore.

Just as governors (Acts 24) and kings (Acts 26) gave the Apostle Paul a hearing, so today the leaders of our nation ought to hear the Word of God.

4. *Crusades have enormous validity because there are people hidden in every city who are searching for God.*

Like Cornelius in Acts 10, they are waiting for God's Good News to come to their attention—but they are lost within the cavernous vastness of our metropolitan areas. Crusade evangelism draws them out of their hiding places! The components of a citywide crusade—mass meetings, radio and television and literature, excited Christians reaching out, and much more—all work together to draw the masses to hear the voice of God speaking from Scripture.

We see this during every crusade. In Miami last March, for instance, a muscular young man named Tyrone was walking aimlessly along the Bayside after ninety-eight days in jail. Someone had given him a Bible, but, having read only parts here and there, he ended up with more questions than answers. He wanted new life; he just didn't know how to get it.

Out on the street without a shirt to his name, Tyrone decided to sit next to a businessman taking in the scenery before going to our crusade meeting at the Knight Center that evening. The businessman invited Tyrone to get a bite to eat and then attend the crusade together.

At the Knight Center, Tyrone silently listened to the gospel message until I gave the invitation. He then stood up and told the businessman in a rather loud voice, "I'm going." At that, Tyrone walked down to the front of the auditorium where he poured out his heart to a counselor, reviewed the gospel basics, and committed his life to Jesus Christ. That night he became a new man!

5. *New generations are constantly coming of age in larger numbers.*

Crusade evangelism touches these large numbers—and the more the better. Even if a city has already been evangelized, in a few years a new set of children will have grown up, and they must be given the opportunity to respond to the Gospel of Christ.

The body of Christ in any given city can never sit quietly by, thinking its evangelistic work is over. Christians who come together for a united crusade are saying, "We are not going to let this generation in our city get away without hearing the claims of Christ. We don't want anyone who lives here in our lifetime to stand later before God's throne and say, 'God, I lived in that city all my life, and no one ever told me about Your Son.'"

This is not a put-down of the local church's ministry and the ongoing daily witness of local believers. Crusade evangelism is personal evangelism multiplied a thousand times. Crusade evangelism complements the local church's outreach. Crusade evangelism meets the need on a scale that a local church cannot. Crusade evangelism stimulates urgency in Christians to carry out their daily witness.

Our command is to evangelize everyone—not just those in our neighborhood or a few select acquaintances with whom we feel comfortable. Everyone in every generation deserves to hear the Gospel.

6. *Neglected duty in the past calls for extraordinary measures now.*

Maybe you feel your church has a strong ministry in outreach and disciple-making and has fulfilled its responsibility. But can you say unquestionably that every person in your city and the surrounding area has heard the Gospel of Jesus Christ? How many in your city have died without ever really knowing God's plan of salvation? How many in your city will die today?

We have been acting in this generation as though we had eternity to evangelize America and the world. But we do not! How long will we wait? Thousands of homes are being destroyed, thousands of young lives are downtrodden and scarred forever, thousands are trapped in a living hell. For how long will we watch this take place until we more aggressively seek to win souls for Christ?

Will we wait until we get more organized? Why should we? God is the master strategist. He knows exactly what He's doing. And if He tells us to proclaim the Gospel, our duty is to obey Him and proclaim it unceasingly.

Why should we be limited by the mistakes of the past? God is perfectly capable of working through His people according to His own desires and in His own special ways to reach each generation. We are not responsible for what the last generation did. But we are responsible for our generation. And remember that crusade evangelism—especially since it stimulates all the other forms of evangelism—can be a glorious instrument used of God to "step into the gap" left by our evangelistic negligence.

7. *Crusade evangelism has a special attraction to youth.*

In crusade after crusade, young people have been the highest-responding age group, though they often seem otherwise indifferent to Christianity. We do well to fully appreciate and utilize a method that has drawing power to those in this choice age of life.

During an evangelistic youth rally in Toronto, a young man named Steve trusted Jesus Christ. When we were back in the city a year later, one of my team members interviewed Steve about his conversion. "I remember that Friday night very well—January 15," he said. "Back then I was suicidal and bitter at life, at my family. I couldn't care about anything. When Luis said come on up, I jumped at the chance. Ever since then I've been witnessing at my school—it's been a joy in my life. And a lot of people have become Christians. What happens is, you tell someone about Jesus, and he becomes a Christian and tells someone else. Miracles happen!" That same night, three more of Steve's friends trusted the Lord at a Youth for Christ rally where I spoke. It was exciting to hear his story and see how God has blessed him with so much fruit.

8. *Though crusade evangelism basically is a matter of harvesting—reaping where others have sown—it also has a soiltesting function.*

Crusade evangelism reveals responsive population groups

so that further church-planting and other efforts can focus on these groups. It indicates where doors are open for the ongoing growth of the church.

Immediately after the fall of communism in Eastern Europe, the newly formed Evangelical Alliance of Romania invited our evangelistic association to preach in several key cities throughout their nation. People were desperate for the Gospel. I've rarely seen people more anxious to experience God's forgiveness. They packed stadium after stadium for weeks. All told, more than 86,500 people committed their lives to Jesus Christ during that explosive series of crusades, and within two years more than 1,100 churches were planted to absorb the still rapidly growing number of people coming to Christ.

9. *Crusade evangelism—practiced in the power of the Holy Spirit and based on the Word of God—helps believers present a strong and united front as the body of Christ to a watching world.*

"Crusade evangelism is a tough proposition today, but we've got to duke it out," says Eddie Gibbs, former professor of evangelism and church renewal at Fuller Theological Seminary. "The bottom line issue for me is this: Periodically, the church has to come together to address the city with the Gospel. That's nonnegotiable. No church can do it on its own."[5]

The confusing divisions within Christianity, especially in the United States, are a scandal, and this confusion calls for united crusades. Let's let America know we love each other and believe the same foundational truths.

The Lord delights to honor the church when it comes together. When barriers are broken down and animosities are buried—and again and again we have seen this happen in a united crusade—then believers experience as never before the love that God has poured into our hearts by the Holy Spirit (Romans 5:5).

Spiritual healing takes place in the body of Christ when God is at work through united crusade evangelism. The truth of the resurrected Christ indwelling each believer comes alive (Galatians 2:20; 1 Corinthians 6). There is a sense of God's presence and blessing in the united efforts of crusade evangelism that are seldom experienced under other circumstances. God's promise in Psalm 133 suddenly becomes vivid: "How good and pleasant it is when brothers live together in unity! . . . For there the Lord bestows his blessing, even life forevermore."

United mass crusades tell the nation that we have a common core of biblical faith that binds us in love both to Jesus Christ and to one another. And that love makes a powerful impression. "By this all men will know that you are my disciples," Jesus said, "if you love one another" (John 13:35).

10. *Crusade evangelism wisely utilized makes it possible to reach the "untouchables" with the Word of God.*

Crusade evangelism that employs all the modern communications media gets past the insulation and isolation of society's higher classes, the professionals, the highly educated, the writers, artists, and entertainers.

One comedian watched me counsel people live on television and decided to host a mock call-in show mimicking me on another station. As he repeatedly listened to tapes of our programs, however, while strenuously trying to learn how to imitate my mannerisms, the message of the Gospel started sinking in. Instead of mocking Christianity, he ended up giving his life to Jesus Christ!

11. *Crusade evangelism provides a historic platform for the prophetic voice of God, speaking through His people, to be heard by a nation.*

By proclaiming God's authoritative Word on a scale that

cannot be ignored, a citywide crusade becomes the moment when the city is forced to confront the living, almighty God. Thus the Gospel can shake a city—even a city numbering millions. And that city can never again be quite the same, because everyone in it knows that the voice of the Lord has been heard. Even stout opponents of the Gospel of Christ must stop to consider it anew—and some are converted.

12. *In the power of the Holy Spirit, crusade evangelism dislodges the powers of darkness.*

There are entrenched forces of darkness that dominate entire cities and nations, forces that cannot be overcome save by the resurrected power of our Lord Jesus Christ. But their strongholds are broken down when the church—in obedience to the commands of Jesus Christ—"moves in" on a city or nation on a massive scale with the proclamation of the Gospel.

By aiming at such a huge block of people, a citywide crusade forces believers to engage in the kind of spiritual warfare that defies the power Satan exercises. That kind of spiritual warfare requires the church to rely on faith, to walk in holiness, to think spiritually and strategically, and to claim the power of the blood of Christ.

13. *A citywide crusade brings rejoicing and celebration to the people of God as they gather by the thousands to hear God's Word proclaimed.*

Even as unbelievers are saved, Christians are lifted up to a great joy. Suddenly they can begin to imagine the magnitude of the celebration awaiting us in heaven, like that described in Revelation—"a great multitude that no one could count, from every nation, tribe, people and language, standing before the throne and in front of the Lamb. . . . And they cried out in a loud voice: 'Salvation belongs to our God, who sits on the throne, and to the Lamb'" (7:9-10).

14. *As believers are trained how to follow up converts*

from the upcoming citywide crusade, the Christian community receives shepherding and counseling.

As Christians prepare to meet the needs of new believers, their own formerly unanswered questions are raised and unmet needs are dealt with. And because this training of crusade workers brings together believers from various segments of the body of Christ, the weaknesses of one segment are balanced out by the strengths of another. In this way the goal expressed in Ephesians 4:12 is acted upon: "to prepare God's people for works of service, so that the body of Christ may be built up."

15. *Time and again, involvement in crusade evangelism revolutionizes the self-image of individual Christians.*

One believer after another is shaken, revived, and transformed. Those who felt discouraged and alone suddenly are excited about the Gospel and about their own unique part in proclaiming it to the world. They feel a sense of belonging and oneness with the whole body of Christ.

16. *Crusade evangelism enhances the image of biblical Christianity.*

Many people think evangelical Christians are mostly ignorant, backward, and foolish. But a successful, momentous crusade leaves a profound impression that honors God and opens up new opportunities for expressing the Gospel of Christ.

17. *Crusade evangelism puts all the gifts of the Holy Spirit to use at every level of human experience, to the glory of God.*

A citywide crusade is an enormous undertaking, but as the responsibility for it is shared by the Christians in that city, their spiritual gifts are mobilized to meet the need. Believers sense the Lord's calling for this hour and that now is the time to serve their Savior with their gifts.

18. *In every citywide crusade, many Christians for the first time in their lives participate in leading an unbeliever to Christ.*

Crusade evangelism provides opportunities for every

Christian to grow and develop in evangelism. The exciting and stimulating atmosphere motivates Christians who have been timid in their witness to launch out in evangelism. When they see the beauty and simplicity of praying with an individual to lead him or her to Christ, they want to have a part in it! For many, their first taste of evangelism through a citywide crusade is the beginning of a lifelong evangelistic ministry. They realize, "This is my city. God has placed me here as His ambassador."

During the San Fernando Valley Crusade in Los Angeles, Linda Oliver counseled several people who received Christ. "I love the Lord," she said, "but I've always been afraid to step out and say something. Now that I've started, don't ever hold me back."

John Tolle, pastor of Living Word Christian Fellowship, said that preparation for the crusade "has mobilized far more Christians who otherwise would be the proverbial Christian couch potatoes. The crusade is leaving behind not just two thousand converts, but thousands of people who are zealous about reaching people for Christ."

19. *Crusade evangelism places the communications media at the service of a sovereign Creator.*

I believe God allowed the invention of modern communications technology for the purpose of sharing His truth. Thus, when television and radio become God's instruments, they fulfill His holy purpose to redeem and bless humanity.

God can use anyone He chooses and anything He pleases to glorify Himself. All creation was made for His glory, and therefore everything is the proper servant of the sovereign God. Thus the mass media can be used to draw the attention of an indifferent, jaded, publicity-drowned public in a big city to the one event that will do them more good than anything else—namely, the preaching of eternal salvation through the Cross, the blood, and the resurrection of Jesus Christ.

20. *Crusade evangelism results in larger churches and new churches.*

I have seen scores of new congregations formed, not to mention the hundreds of existing churches that experienced solid growth from the fruit of mass evangelistic efforts.

During eleven days of crusade meetings in Tulsa and Stillwater, Oklahoma, more than 1,340 people made commitments to Christ. No one was more excited than Victor Orta, a Baptist church planter. As a result of the campaign, Victor said he'll be busy planting three churches.

The sheer volume of new converts through the sovereign action of the Holy Spirit is the most obvious reason for this most desirable result. But mass campaigns can also enlarge the vision of church leaders for ongoing church growth and church-planting endeavors.

21. *Many receive a call to full-time Christian ministry as a result of mass evangelistic campaigns.*

This is especially true for young people. Having tasted the excitement of a massive citywide crusade, they are not content to settle for anything less in their life work than wholehearted service to the cause of the Gospel.

22. *Crusade evangelism acts as the catalyst for many other forms of evangelism and Bible teaching.*

Crusades open doors for ministry that might be opened no other way. Believers become more willing and daring to initiate new and different methods of ministry and evangelism. We've seen this all across Europe and Latin America, in parts of Asia, and here in America as well.

In one prominent Asian city, we faced unexpected opposition to our plans to set aside one meeting especially to reach children with the Gospel. We discovered intense cultural opposition to the idea of proclaiming the Good News of Jesus Christ to kids. With extreme reluctance, the crusade executive committee finally agreed to proceed with the event. It went against their better judgment—until they saw more than sixteen thousand children trust Christ that day!

23. *The public confession of faith in Christ reinforces the decision of commitment.*

During a crusade thousands of people commit their lives publicly to Christ. By making this step of faith in the presence of a multitude, a new believer's inner action before God is strengthened. Hundreds are watching—his neighbors, friends, relatives, and others—as he surrenders his life to Christ, and thus he is opening up his soul not only to God but also to the entire body of Christ. The carefully planned follow-up ministry further reinforces the individual's decision.

Just as the apostles called for public, visible baptism, and just as the people of Israel raised stone altars to express their dedication to God, so in crusade evangelism the public response to the Gospel speaks volumes.

24. *Crusade evangelism creates the climate for calls to justice and honesty at all levels of national life.*

This climate opens the door for the body of Christ to influence society as the salt of the earth and the light of the world. As thousands are converted to Christ and see their personal, family, and vocational life transformed, a city and nation are affected economically, politically, and socially.

The more people who become converted, the greater effect on society. Thus, proclaiming the Gospel leads to fundamental social advancement.

"Never is it the quantity of decisions that determines the destiny of a group of people," said Jack Hayford, senior pastor of Church on the Way, during the San Fernando Valley Crusade. "It's individuals who determine the destiny. Any handful of them, or any one of them, could become an instrument to determine for good the destiny of our city. They're certainly going to determine for good the destiny of hundreds or thousands of families and businesses. To have a couple of thousand individuals changed is going to impact hundreds of thousands of people."

25. *Crusade evangelism leads to revival—spiritual renewal and strengthening—within the church.*

Few if any revivals in church history have happened apart from major evangelistic movements. Again and again it has been shown that active evangelism produces revival in the church, and the record of citywide crusades provides strong evidence for this. The backslidden are brought back, the immature are built up, the old-timers are encouraged, the ministers are strengthened.

During one of our crusades, a Lutheran minister realized: "I had been preaching evangelism, but not practicing it." Just prior to the crusade, he had taken our evangelistic association's Bridgebuilder training courses in friendship evangelism, counseling, and follow-up. In eleven years of full-time ministry up to that point, he had to admit he had led only one person to Jesus Christ—and he has doubts about that one.

During a pre-marital counseling session about a week after the crusade, however, this pastor asked the young couple if they had eternal life. They said no. Instead of just talking to them about their need to trust Jesus Christ, he invited them to make that decision right there in his office. Within six months, he had led more than twenty other people to Christ.

What began as renewal in one pastor's life has produced a fabulous breakthrough in his church. And God has given him opportunities to help other churches experience spiritual and numerical growth. "I don't think my feet have hit the ground yet," he remarked. "This is the beginning of a real revival for our congregation."

26. *Finally, crusade evangelism glorifies God and thus is pleasing in His sight.*

Crusade evangelism glorifies God because it proclaims the holiness of His name; it exalts the person and work of His Son; it communicates God's grace in providing for our salvation through Christ's substitutionary death on the cross and His powerful resurrection from the dead; it proclaims God's power to transform individuals, families, cities, and nations; it warns of His judgment to come; and it holds forth our living hope of dwelling eternally with God in heaven. All this is done before the multitudes.

God's heart is pleased when the fragrance of the knowledge of Him is thus spread everywhere. And as others have said, success is anything that is pleasing to God. Even if none were converted—though of course many thousands are—crusade evangelism would be a worthy pursuit because it exalts God before the masses. What a thrilling experience!

Does crusade evangelism have a future in America? My answer is a resounding "Yes!" Why? Because God blesses that which truly glorifies Himself.

From our human perspective, this is all that really counts. We do it for Him. And I believe that those who practice crusade evangelism now and in the future will be moved to exclaim with the Apostle Paul, "Now to the King eternal, immortal, invisible, the only God, be honor and glory for ever and ever. Amen" (1 Timothy 1:17).

TO PONDER

1. Read Acts 2:14, 36-41 again. The morning of Pentecost, when the church first came into existence, God drew a huge crowd around the small group of Christians.

What did the Holy Spirit prompt the Apostle Peter to do? What was the result?

2. "Just as in the days of most of the revivals recorded in history, mass evangelism remains and will remain one of the most powerful tools that God has placed in our hands." Why is mass evangelism particularly effective in this generation?

3. "While one-on-one evangelism is crucial, it's impossible to win the world to Jesus Christ one person at a time. People are born into this world and die faster than we can reach them unless we take advantage of a multiplicity of methods to reach the masses." According to the book of Acts, what methods did the apostles use to proclaim the Gospel? Which bore fruit? Which should we use today?

4. "The body of Christ in any given city can never sit quietly by, thinking its evangelistic work is over." Why not?

5. "Crusade evangelism is personal evangelism multiplied a thousand times." How does a united, citywide evangelistic crusade stimulate and multiply the witness of local churches and individuals?

6. "We have been acting in this generation as though we had eternity to evangelize America and the world. But we do not!" What are some common excuses for not organizing massive evangelistic outreaches? What are some of the tragic results when we hesitate to proclaim the Gospel to the masses?

7. "Few if any revivals in church history have happened apart from major evangelistic movements." If that's true, what do we need before we experience another significant revival in America?

8

GOD'S
OBSESSION

Woe to me if I do not preach the gospel!

— 1 Corinthians 9:16

8

DOES GOD HAVE AN *OBSESSION?* That's probably not the right word to describe the Lord's preoccupation with saving sinners. The Bible calls it *love*. But it's such an incomprehensible, unreasonable love. Jesus said, "Greater love has no one than this, that he lay down his life for his friends" (John 15:13). When Jesus laid down His life on the cross, the men He called His friends deserted Him.

No greater love? When Jesus Christ died for our sins, it wasn't only for the sins of Peter, James, John, Martha, and Mary. "You see, at just the right time, when we were still powerless, Christ died for the ungodly. Very rarely will anyone die for a righteous man, though for a good man someone might possibly dare to die. But God demonstrates his own love for us in this: While we were still sinners, Christ died for us. Since we have now been justified by his blood, how much more shall we be saved from God's wrath through him! For if, when we were God's enemies, we were reconciled to him through the death of his Son, how much more, having been reconciled, shall we be saved through his life" (Romans 5:6-10).

"Surely he took up our infirmities and carried our sorrows, yet we considered him stricken by God, smitten by him, and afflicted. But he was pierced for our transgressions, he was crushed for our iniquities; the punishment that brought us peace was upon him, and by his wounds we are healed. We all, like sheep, have gone astray, each of us has turned to his own way; and the Lord has laid on him the iniquity of us all" (Isaiah 53:4-6).

"How great is the love the Father has lavished on us, that we should be called children of God!" (1 John 3:1).

ZEAL FOR THE GOSPEL

This love snared one of God's foremost enemies, Saul of Tarsus, as he was en route to Damascus to persecute more followers of Jesus. Saul became Paul, self-described as "the worst of sinners," apostle to the Gentiles: "Here is a trustworthy saying that deserves full acceptance: Christ Jesus came into the world to save sinners—of whom I am the worst. But for that very reason I was shown mercy so that in me, the worst of sinners, Christ Jesus might display his unlimited patience as an example for those who would believe on him and receive eternal life" (1 Timothy 1:15-16).

What the Apostle Paul endured for the sake of the Gospel of Jesus Christ puts me to shame. With apologies to Henry Varley, who said to D. L. Moody, "Moody, the world has yet to see what God will do with a man fully consecrated to Him," I believe Paul was such a man. He served God "with [his] whole heart in preaching the Gospel of his Son" (Romans 1:9).

• Five times Paul received forty lashes minus one.

• Three times he was beaten with rods.

• Once he was stoned.

• Three times he was shipwrecked.

• He spent a night and a day in the open sea.

• He faced danger everywhere: from rivers, from bandits, from Jews and Gentiles, from false brothers; danger in the city, in the country, at sea.

• He often went without sleep, food, and water, and he knew what it was like to be cold and naked (2 Corinthians 11:24-27).

"Though I am free and belong to no man, I make myself a slave to everyone, to win as many as possible. To the Jews I became like a Jew, to win the Jews. To those under the law I became like one under the law (though I myself am not under the law), so as to win those under the law. To those not having the law I became like one not having the law (though I am not free from God's law but am under Christ's law), so as to win those not having the law. To the weak I became weak, to win the weak. I have become all things to all men so that by all possible means I might save some. I do all this for the sake of the gospel, that I may share in its blessings" (1 Corinthians 9:19-23).

Paul was obsessed with the Gospel. He was a Christian of zeal.

MISDIRECTED VIRTUE

Zeal hasn't disappeared from the lives of American Christians; it's simply misdirected in confused priorities. Every weekend of autumn, for example, check out the nation's football stadiums.

Probably no individual personifies zeal better than the football coach—the one who sleeps on a cot in his office five days a week so he can devote twenty hours a day devising and implementing a strategy to defeat his next opponent.

In America zeal for football makes perfect sense. But zeal for God—and those things that matter most to Him—is too often misunderstood and criticized as "fanaticism," "excessive," or, worse, "extremism."

Sports Illustrated published a perfect illustration in its profile of Bill McCartney, who had just resigned as football coach at the University of Colorado.[1] Most Christians know McCartney better as founder of Promise Keepers, the fast-growing men's movement. He quit, he said, to spend more time with his wife. The magazine article quoted a friend saying that thirty years of putting football first had left McCartney "trying to play catch-up with his family."

"I see an opportunity to put everything on a back burner and have a marriage become all it's capable of being," the coach said. "That's what's in my heart and nothing else."

The article's coauthors struggled to understand. "What man gives up such power and prestige? . . . Put another way, what man walks out on a $350,000-per-year contract with ten years remaining? So that he can spend time with his wife and his god?"

Throughout the article the authors use terms such as "gone nuts," "weird religious mission," "radical," "gone off his head," "fervor," "passion," "single-minded," "devotion," "consumed," and, of course, "religious zealot" to describe McCartney and his ideas. Everything short of "fanatic."

They're describing a person of zeal, an asset for football coaches, but too often considered a liability for people with religious inclinations. A little bit of God is politically correct, but zeal for the Lord could make you an extremist.

The Bible does warn of "zeal without knowledge," but it clearly defines zeal as a virtue to pursue. "Never be lacking in zeal," Paul commands, "but keep your spiritual fervor, serving the Lord" (Romans 12:11).

Zeal is often associated with youth. A young person who has just discovered a personal relationship with Jesus Christ usually becomes an instant evangelist. He or she is like Peter and John after the day of Pentecost. Warned by the religious authorities to stop talking about Jesus, the two disciples replied, "Judge for yourselves whether it is right in God's sight to obey you rather than God. For we cannot help speaking about what we have seen and heard" (Acts 4:19-20).

But for most Christians, this zeal for the Gospel and the boldness that goes with it disappears far too early in life. Perhaps because they fear being considered "fools for Christ" (1 Corinthians 4:10). Fanatics. Religious zealots.

SWEATING IT OUT FOR GOD

Zeal can be misguided. As a virtue in isolation, it can lead to distortion of the truth, anger, and pride. As a young man eager to win souls for Christ, I had dedicated and rededicated my life to Christ probably a dozen times. Every time I took off with great zeal and high expectations, only to come crashing back down in failure.

The problem was that I was zealously trying to sweat it out for God. Always trying to overcome temptation by sheer dedication, discipline, Bible study, prayer, and hard, zealous gospel work. My friends and I tried just about everything to win people to Christ—sharp-looking tracts, evangelistic radio programs, enthusiastic street meetings. Some would listen; others would ridicule. But we saw few trust Jesus Christ as Savior.

Then some of my closest friends fell away from the Lord.

Not completely at first, but they cooled off. Eventually our all-Friday-night prayer meetings dried up, too.

Up to then I had been self-confident and ego-centered. "God, You really got Yourself a prize in me. I tell You, I'm going to be dedicated till death. If I have to die for the kingdom, I'll do it." In my heart was a feeling that "I'm going to show the world—and Henry Varley—what a young man can do for God."

It was "zeal without knowledge." God could hardly wait for me to admit I couldn't live for Him by sheer determination. It's futile trying to please God in our own strength. But, praise the Lord, He is pleased to live in us! This is the fact that changed my life: we're united with Christ, and He wants to manifest His resurrection life through you and me. "I have been crucified with Christ and I no longer live, but Christ lives in me" (Galatians 2:20).[2]

Zeal motivated by that central truth is costly because it requires sacrifice, a willingness to go anywhere, give up anything, and endure all things for Jesus, while relying on His indwelling resurrection life. Paul's own life is ample proof.

Jesus, of course, is our perfect example. In His zeal for the salvation of the world, God's one and only Son left heaven for earth, "taking the very nature of a servant, being made in human likeness. And being found in appearance as a man, he humbled himself and became obedient to death—even death on a cross!" (Philippians 2:7-8).

THE REAL TEST OF ZEAL

I believe that zeal will show itself in evangelism; a zealous Christian will be a zealous witness for Christ.[3] It's true, because people are God's priority. "There is nothing more important to

God than rescuing what He created," says my friend and fellow evangelist Clyde Dupin.

Jesus defined His mission clearly: "For the Son of Man came to seek and to save what was lost" (Luke 19:10). And He commands all of us to go and tell everyone.

I believe Bill McCartney is a Christian of zeal, certainly zeal for his family, but also zeal for evangelism. One of the "Seven Promises of Promise Keepers" is: "A Promise Keeper is committed to influencing his world, being obedient to the Great Commandment and the Great Commission." Every Promise Keepers conference proclaims the Gospel and invites men to commit their lives to Jesus Christ. Tens of thousands have done so.

Helen Roseveare is a Christian of zeal. A missionary doctor in the Belgian Congo (now Zaire) during a civil war in 1964, Helen was captured by rebel soldiers, beaten, and raped. After her release and furlough, however, Helen returned to her work in Zaire for seven more years.

"I want people to be passionately in love with Jesus, so that nothing else counts," Helen said. "Maybe God calls me to Africa in the midst of an area being swept by a killer disease that no one knows how to cure. What if I get AIDS—or my spouse or children? The world thinks I'm foolish for going there. But if God sent me to Africa with my family, he's going to look after us.

"That doesn't mean I'm not going to get that disease; it means that he's in charge of my life, and if I get AIDS, that's because he wants me to witness to others who've got it. How's that for success?

"I'm a fanatic, if you like, but only because I believe so strongly that nothing counts except knowing your sins have been forgiven by the blood of Jesus. We've only got this short life to get others to know the same truth."[4]

Nothing is more important to God than rescuing what He created. All of us need a constantly renewed tenderness, a continual firing up from God, a revived love for those who suffer and who die without Jesus. I don't know how long God will give me on this earth, but I am asking Him for a greater and greater passion for the souls of people who still live in selfishness and sinfulness, who are on their way to eternal perdition. This is the example our Lord Jesus Christ has left us.

Let us therefore commit ourselves to give every ounce of our energy in obedient service to our Lord, as we keep to the goal of fully evangelizing our generation. May this become our obsession.[5]

TO PONDER

1. Read 1 Corinthians 9:16 again. If God so loves the world, how should we express that love? Dare we not express it?

2. "Paul was obsessed with the Gospel. He was a Christian of zeal." What did he endure to proclaim the Gospel throughout the known world? What did he do to reach as many people as possible?

3. "Zeal hasn't disappeared from the lives of American Christians; it's simply misdirected in confused priorities." In addition to football, what are many Americans zealous about? In light of eternity, do any of these things merit such time, energy, and passion?

4. "The Bible does warn of 'zeal without knowledge,' but it clearly defines zeal as a virtue to pursue." Who tend to be the most zealous for God and bold to proclaim the Gospel to others? What often happens to such zeal? Why?

5. "As a virtue in isolation, zeal can lead to distortion of the truth, anger, and pride." What misconceptions can lead to such distortions? According to Galatians 2:20, what is the real source of our strength as Christians?

6. "Zeal motivated by that central truth [that 'Christ lives in me'] is costly because it requires sacrifice, a willingness to go anywhere, give up anything, and endure all things for Jesus, while relying on His indwelling resurrection life." Who in the New Testament best exemplifies godly zeal?

7. "I believe that zeal will show itself in evangelism; a zealous Christian will be a zealous witness for Christ." What did Jesus say was His mission on earth? How zealous was He to fulfill that mission? What is Jesus' commission to us? How zealous will we be to help fulfill His Great Commission in our generation?

9

NAILED
BY THE GOSPEL

We are therefore Christ's ambassadors,
as though God were making his appeal
through us. We implore you on
Christ's behalf: Be reconciled to God.

— 2 Corinthians 5:20

9

ON A FLIGHT FROM BUDAPEST to London, a British Christian woman was witnessing to a Hungarian businesswoman sitting next to her. One row back, our evangelistic association's European director and I were discussing the evangelistic rally we'd had in Budapest the day before with British pop star Cliff Richard.

While we were talking, the Christian woman stood up, turned around and said, "Excuse me. Are you talking about the rally yesterday with Cliff Richard and Luis Palau?" I said yes. "Do you know where brother Palau is?" I said that was me. Then she said, "I've been talking to this Hungarian lady, and I think she's ready to be converted. But I don't know how to do it."

I told her, "I've been listening to what you've been saying, and you've done a terrific job." But she feared doing something wrong when it came to praying with someone ready to receive

Jesus Christ. So I agreed to talk with the Hungarian businesswoman for a minute.

"Did you understand what this lady said to you?" I
asked.

"Yes," said the woman.

"Are you ready to open the door of your life to Jesus
Christ?"

"Yes."

At that, I asked the Christian woman to lead her in a
prayer of decision and sat back down. I would have loved to
have led her to Christ myself; it would have been great.
Instead, I sat back and watched as the Christian woman in
front of me at first hesitated, then put her arm around this
Hungarian woman, and for the first time led someone to
Jesus Christ.

If we don't give an actual invitation to receive Jesus
Christ, we haven't presented the whole Gospel. The
Gospel is ultimately a call from God, an invitation for the
listener to believe, to surrender, to trust Jesus Christ for
salvation.

When the Apostle Paul stood before King Agrippa (Acts
26), he made very clear that God had called him not only to
preach His Son, but also to lead people to decide for Jesus
Christ. Paul recounted events on the road to Damascus, sum-
marized his mission to the Gentiles, and then pressed the
king for a decision. "'King Agrippa, do you believe the
prophets? I know you do.' Then Agrippa said to Paul, 'Do
you think that in such a short time you can persuade me to
be a Christian?'

"'Short time or long—I pray God that not only you but
all who are listening to me today may become what I am,
except for these chains.'"

INVITATIONS IN SCRIPTURE

From Genesis 3 on, the Bible is God's invitation to the fallen human race. After he sinned, Adam hid from God, who called him back: "Adam, where are you?" Consider just a few of the invitation verses of Scripture:

"Repent, for the kingdom of heaven is near" (Matthew 4:17).

"Come to me, all you who are weary and burdened" (Matthew 11:28).

"Tell those who have been invited that I have prepared my dinner. . . . Come to the wedding banquet" (Matthew 22:4).

"Go to the street corners and invite to the banquet anyone you find" (Matthew 22:9).

"I have not come to call the righteous, but sinners to repentance" (Luke 5:32).

"Zacchaeus, come down immediately. I must stay at your house today" (Luke 19:5).

"If anyone is thirsty, let him come to me and drink" (John 7:37).

"Repent and be baptized, every one of you, in the name of Jesus Christ for the forgiveness of your sins" (Acts 2:38).

"Repent, then, and turn to God, so that your sins may be wiped out, that times of refreshing may come from the Lord" (Acts 3:19).

"The Lord is not slow in keeping his promise, as some understand slowness. He is patient with you, not wanting anyone to perish, but everyone to come to repentance" (2 Peter 3:9).

And perhaps the most touching invitation in Scripture: "The Spirit and the bride say, 'Come!' And let him who hears say, 'Come!' Whoever is thirsty, let him come; and whoever wishes, let him take the free gift of the water of life" (Revelation 22:17).

HOW DO YOU OPEN THE DOOR?

An evangelist is a doorman. He stands at the door of the kingdom and calls to all the masses of people passing by, "Come in, come in, come in! This is the only door—come in here!"

At a welcoming party for Mission to London in 1984, I sat beside a member of the royal family. When all the niceties were over, the first thing she said was, "Dr. Palau, I have wanted to talk to an evangelist for years and years. I have two questions. First, do you have the assurance of eternal life? And if you do, how did you come about it? And if one wanted to have this assurance, how would one go about it? Can you help me?"

"Yes, your royal highness, I think I can help," I said. To be brief, I used the gospel presentation that Child Evangelism Fellowship workers taught me when I was a teenager in Argentina. I quoted several verses, including 1 John 5:11-12: "God has given us eternal life, and this life is in his Son. He who has the Son has life; he who does not have the Son of God does not have life."

She said, "But how do I get the Son of God if I want life?"

"Ma'am, the Bible says, 'Yet to all who received him, to those who believed in his name, he gave the right to become children of God'" (John 1:12).

She said, "Receive Him? How do you receive Him?"

"Ma'am, in the Bible Jesus says, 'I stand at the door and knock. If anyone hears my voice and opens the door, I will come in and eat with him, and he with me'" (Revelation 3:20).

She said, "Open the door? How do you open the door?"

"It's as if I go to your residence later this afternoon and knock on the door. You look out the window and say to your husband, 'Oh dear, it's Palau. What are we going to do? He talks too much. Do we let him in?' Jesus is knocking at the door of your heart. Open your heart; let Him come in. The way to let Him in is to ask Him to come in."

That's my favorite invitation illustration, which I've used hundreds of times in evangelistic meetings to show people how to receive Christ.

MY TURN TO DECIDE

Jesus said over and over, "Come. Drink. Eat. Receive. Follow Me. Repent." On many occasions He gave His listeners a clear opportunity to choose between surrender or rebellion, light or darkness, hope or despair. So should you—with friends and neighbors, the children's Sunday school class you teach, the Bible study you lead.

A British missionary, Frank Chandler, led me to Jesus Christ at summer camp when I was twelve years old. I was a nasty little fellow—not tough, just nasty—and I needed a counselor like Mr. Chandler. Each evening of camp he took a boy from our tent outside, walked a short ways, sat down, went over the gospel basics, and gave him an opportunity to say yes or no to Christ.

Finally, the last night of camp, my turn came. He sat me down on a log, opened his New Testament, and pulled out a flashlight. "Luis, you've got to make a decision tonight. If you die tonight, are you going to heaven or hell?" Just like that, straight out.

I hesitated, then replied, "I'm going to hell."

"Do you want to go there?" he asked.

"No."

"Then why are you going there?"

"I don't know."

"Do you know what you need to do not to go there?" he asked.

"Yes," I said. "'Believe in the Lord Jesus Christ, and you shall be saved.'"

"Wait, wait, wait," he said, and he turned to Romans 10:9-10. He inserted my name, as R. A. Torrey taught. "'If you, Luis, confess with your lips that Jesus is Lord and believe in your heart, Luis, that God raised Him from the dead, you, Luis, shall be saved.' You understand that?" he asked.

"I understand."

"Do you believe in your heart that God raised Jesus from the dead?"

"Yes, I do."

"What do you have to do?"

"Confess Him with my lips."

"Are you going to do it or not?"

"Yes."

Mr. Chandler put his arm around me—it was beginning to rain, and he was in a hurry—and said to me, "Okay, you're going to pray and confess with your lips." And I did. He led me phrase by phrase: "Oh, God (Oh, God), I deserve to go to hell (I deserve to go to hell). Thank You that Jesus died (Thank You that Jesus died). I receive You in my heart (I receive You in my heart). Now I have eternal life (Now I have eternal life). Amen."

I was saved forever that night. I thank God that Mr. Chandler was a tough guy, that he didn't try to finesse me into the kingdom. He just nailed this nasty twelve-year-old boy with a direct invitation to receive Jesus Christ.

GIVE A CLEAR INVITATION

Use any method you want, as long as it's ethical and clear. One good approach is Evangelism Explosion's two questions:

"Have you come to the place in your spiritual life where you know for certain that if you were to die today, you would go to heaven?" and "Suppose you were to die today and stand before God and He were to say to you, 'Why should I let you into My heaven?' What would you say?" Most Americans say good works will get them into heaven. Don't argue with them. Just give them the Gospel, show them from the Bible all about the good news of God's grace, and then go back to Evangelism Explosion's second question and their answer. Contrast what they think with what God's Word declares. Then invite them to trust Christ, praying with you right then and there.

When I counsel someone after the invitation, I often use Paul Little's questions. I ask, "Have you trusted Jesus Christ yet, or are you still on the way?" It's a great question because the moment people answer, you usually know if they're in the kingdom or out. But it doesn't put them on the spot. If the person I'm counseling says, "I'm still on the way," I ask, "How far along the way?" That usually reveals how well he understands the gospel message. The third question is, "Would you like to receive Jesus Christ right now?" If he's ready, I discuss the gospel basics and lead him in a prayer.

The Wordless Book, which uses color pages without words to communicate the gospel basics, also is an effective evangelistic tool with children and in cross-cultural settings.

The main thing is to actually invite people to open the door, to repent and believe. God commands a response to His gift of love, His one and only Son. Without an invitation, our blossoming evangelistic efforts will never reach fruition.

Here in America, we're losing the battle for souls because the church is not giving a clear invitation. We are confused about what evangelism really is. Conversions are not automatic, and the Gospel is not just information. The Gospel is an invitation. Unbelievers must face a dilemma:

"What am I going to do with Christ?" Pastors and preachers of the Gospel call for people to make a decision for Jesus Christ. John Stott says, "This decision to receive Jesus Christ by faith is first a definite act." Without this invitation, you haven't preached the Gospel.

The Lausanne Covenant contains an outstanding statement on evangelism: "To evangelize is to spread the good news that Jesus Christ died for our sins and was raised from the dead according to the Scriptures, and that as the reigning Lord He now offers the forgiveness of sins and the liberating gift of the Spirit to all who repent and believe. Our Christian presence in the world is indispensable to evangelism, and so is that kind of dialogue whose purpose is to listen sensitively in order to understand. But evangelism itself is the proclamation of the historical, biblical Christ as Savior and Lord, with a view to persuading people to come to Him personally and to be reconciled to God. In issuing the Gospel invitation we have no liberty to conceal the cost of discipleship. Jesus still calls all who would follow Him to deny themselves, take up their cross, and identify themselves with His new community. The results of evangelism include obedience to Christ, incorporation into His church, and responsible service in the world."

What a privilege it is to invite people to be reconciled to God. We need to confront unbelievers as Jesus did, with compassion and love (Mark 10:21), so they won't close their ears or heart to God's voice. I find that many people want to know what steps to take to respond to Christ. Ours is the pleasure of telling them quite specifically and simply.

So be bold. Be persistent. Be faithful to give an invitation. The Lord will give you fruit, and it will be your joy and crown in heaven.

"We shall have all eternity in which to celebrate our victories," Robert Moffat said, "but we have only one swift hour before the sunset in which to win the lost to Christ."

TO PONDER

1. Read 2 Corinthians 5:20 again. Who are Christ's ambassadors? What is our central message?

2. "If we don't give an actual invitation to receive Jesus Christ, we haven't presented the whole Gospel." Why not?

3. "From Genesis 3 on, the Bible is God's invitation to the fallen human race." What are some of the most famous invitation passages?

4. "An evangelist is a doorman. He stands at the door of the kingdom and calls to all the masses of people passing by, 'Come in, come in, come in! This is the only door—come in here!'" Where are you most likely to see a doorman, and why? What are a doorman's most important duties? How is an evangelist's job similar? Different?

5. "On many occasions Jesus gave His listeners a clear opportunity to choose between surrender and rebellion, light or darkness, hope or despair." When were you first invited to commit your life to Jesus Christ? Did you respond that day? If so, how much had you heard about the Gospel previously? If you did not respond, how much longer did you wait to trust Christ?

6. "Without an invitation, our blossoming evangelistic efforts will never reach fruition." What method should you use to present an invitation?

7. "Here in America, we're losing the battle for souls because the church is not giving a clear invitation. We are confused about what evangelism really is. Conversions are not automatic, and the Gospel is not just information." What dilemma must unbelievers face? What is our part in making them aware of that dilemma and encouraging them to choose new life in Jesus Christ? What is God's part?

_10_

DREAM GREAT DREAMS

"I tell you the truth, anyone who has faith in me will do what I have been doing. He will do even greater things than these, because I am going to the Father. And I will do whatever you ask in my name, so that the Son may bring glory to the Father. You may ask me for anything in my name, and I will do it. If you love me, you will obey what I command."

— John 14:12-15

10

HAVE YOU EVER TASTED A NICE, COOL, refreshing Coke? Congratulations! So have hundreds of millions of other people all around the world. And it's all Robert Woodruff's fault.

Well, not all his fault. But he's largely to blame.

You see, Woodruff served as president of Coca-Cola from 1923 to 1955. While chief executive of that soft drink corporation, he had the audacity to state, "We will see that every man in uniform gets a bottle of Coca-Cola for five cents wherever he is and whatever it costs."

After World War II ended, he went on to say that in his lifetime he wanted *everyone* in the world to have a taste of Coca-Cola. Talk about vision!

With careful planning and a lot of persistence, Woodruff and his colleagues reached their generation around the globe for Coke.

Say, how big is your vision? Have you ever thought

about what God could do through you to influence our own generation?

I'm not kidding. Neither was the Lord Jesus Christ kidding when He called His disciples to gain a vision of impacting the world for His name.

The Twelve (minus Judas) listened intently as Christ sought to prepare them for His imminent betrayal and subsequent death.

"No matter what happens," He told them, "believe in Me. I am the Way and the Truth and the Life. I am in the Father and He is in Me. We work in unity. If you can't believe My words alone, at least believe Me because of the miracles you have seen."

Then the Lord startled the apostles with the words of John 14:12-15, quoted above. Don't underestimate those words. Read them again. Here in capsule form Christ challenges His disciples—and that now includes you and me—to dream great dreams, plan great plans, pray great prayers, and obey His great commands.

DREAM GREAT DREAMS

In the disciples' minds, time was fast running out. For more than three years they had hoped that Christ would be the one who would redeem Israel and reign as Messiah. But now He was saying that one of them would betray Him and deliver Him up to the Jewish leaders to be crucified.

They couldn't accept what He was telling them: "I will be with you only a little longer. . . . I am going to the Father. . . . I am leaving you." Everything within them screamed, "No! This can't be true!"

So imagine what the Twelve thought when Christ went on

to promise, "I tell you the truth, anyone who has faith in me will do what I have been doing" (John 14:12a).

Around the upper room table sat Peter, who had almost drowned trying to walk on water. And Philip, who waved his arms in exclamation when stating the impossibility of buying enough bread to feed the multitude. And Andrew, who with a number of the other disciples could not even heal a boy who was demon-possessed.

To each disciple Christ said, "You can continue the work I have been doing." And His promise is the same to you and me. He calls us to dream great dreams of what we can do to impact our world for His glory. How is this possible? The key is twofold.

First, because Christ was going to the Father, He assured the disciples that He would send the Comforter, the Holy Spirit, to indwell all believers. Christ would now continue His work through us!

Second, Christ qualified His promise with a condition. Notice that He said, "Anyone who has faith in me will do what I have been doing." The Lord challenges us to have faith—not necessarily more faith, but to have faith in Him. It is an ongoing faith. The Williams translation puts it this way: "Whoever perseveres in believing in me can himself do the things that I am doing."

Have you stopped seeing great things happen in your life? Perhaps you have stopped believing that God can work in a mighty way in our generation. But what limits the work of God here on earth? Is God somehow incapable of renewing the churches in America? Of turning the hearts of multiplied thousands to Himself? Of causing the fires of revival to spread throughout this country and beyond? Of course not! Yet God has chosen to limit His works, at least in some measure, to those things we trust Him to do through us.

Why is it that so few Christians ever accomplish great things for Christ? I believe it is because we lose the ability to dream great dreams. You see it happening all the time.

New believers are notorious for their enthusiasm and almost childlike trust in God. Accounts of such heroes of the faith as George Müller, Hudson Taylor, Corrie ten Boom, and Dawson Trotman inspire them to step out and attempt what others consider presumptuous.

But as time goes by, hardening of the spiritual arteries sets in, and we become cynical. We lose the joy and thrill of the Christian life. We hear of something wonderful happening and say, "Oh?" as if it were really nothing. How nonchalant we become about God's work around the world!

Oh, our doctrinal statements still sound theologically correct, but our lives deny the reality we profess.

In order for God to use us again, we need to confess our unbelief and say: "Lord Jesus, renew my vision of Your power. Renew my confidence in Your abilities. Renew my trust in Your resources." Then begin to dream again!

Christ Himself never limited His disciples' vision. Even though He restricted His own public ministry to Palestine, He came and lived and died for all mankind. And after His resurrection, He commissioned His followers to "make disciples of all nations" (Matthew 28:19) and sent them first to Jerusalem, then to all Judea and Samaria, and ultimately to the ends of the earth (Acts 1:8).

But the early church did what we all do—they hesitated to dream about what God wanted to do in their own generation. It finally took the stoning of Stephen and subsequent conversion of Saul to shake them out of their complacency.

While other believers scattered throughout Palestine, the Apostle Paul took Christ's Great Commission seriously and devoted the latter half of his life to traveling and proclaiming the Gospel to the Gentiles.

In Romans 15 Paul records a summary of his first missionary journey. He had already given detailed oral reports to the church in Antioch (see Acts 14:27) and to the Jerusalem Council (Acts 15:12). But here he simply states, "From Jerusalem all the way around to Illyricum, I have fully proclaimed the gospel of Christ" (Romans 15:19).

Now, the distance from Jerusalem to Illyricum is some 750 miles over land. Yet Paul could look back on that trip and say, "Mission accomplished. I have fully proclaimed the Gospel in that entire area." Paul didn't stop, however, and assume there wasn't anything left to do. Instead, he was already dreaming of the mission fields beyond.

Where have your own dreams stopped? Have they been lost somewhere between your living room and the house next door? If your dreams aren't greater than finishing your education, paying your bills, or raising your children, then your vision isn't divine. Maybe it's time to consider how God could use you to make a difference in the lives of others.

Opportunities to serve Christ abound if we take God at His word and plan to accomplish great things by His power working through us.

PLAN GREAT PLANS

When I was about seventeen years old and beginning to take the Word of God seriously, John 14:12 really bothered me. I just couldn't believe what the second half of the verse says. I even checked other translations to see if I could find a better rendering. But the verse reads essentially the same in each version.

Jesus Christ declares, "He [who believes in me] will do

even greater things than these [which I have done], because I am going to the Father" (John 14:12b).

That is a fantastic, almost incredible, yet true promise. It came from the lips of the Lord Jesus and has been proved trustworthy many times. Christ promises that we can do *greater* works than He did!

Perhaps another look at the ministry of Paul will help us better understand what Christ is saying here. Without a doubt, God used Paul tremendously during the crucial, formative years of the New Testament church. Even his opponents admitted that Paul had saturated entire provinces with the Gospel (Acts 19:26) and turned the world upside down (Acts 17:6).

Some scholars have even claimed that, from a human point of view, this Pharisee-turned-preacher influenced history more than Jesus Christ Himself. In his book *From Guilt to Glory*, Ray Stedman says, "Did you ever stop to ask yourself what influence the Apostle Paul has had in your own life? He lived nearly two thousand years ago, and yet there is not one person among us who has not had his life drastically affected by this man. The whole course of history has been changed by the truths he taught."[1]

Now would you like your church to support a missionary like *that*?

What was Paul's secret? Simple. He wasn't just a dreamer. He also planned great plans and carried them out in the power of the Holy Spirit. Those plans included utilizing ministry teams, traveling extensively, taking advantage of opportunities to witness for Christ, and establishing local churches to nurture new believers.

You see, Paul wasn't content to saturate one small area with the Gospel at the expense of the rest of the world. He had a strategy for reaching the entire Roman Empire! He could say, "But now that there is no more place for me to work in these regions [Jerusalem to Illyricum], and since I have been longing for many years to see you [in Rome], I plan to do so when I go to Spain" (Romans 15:23-24).

Paul goes on in that chapter to explain his itinerary. In his mind he could visualize every major city he would stop at on his way to Rome. He longed to eventually win the people of that capital city to Christ. But beyond that, his ultimate goal was to reach Spain—the western limit of the empire.

Notice that the apostle used strategic thinking to fulfill his ministry. He didn't consider it carnal or beneath his dignity to plan strategically. Instead, he used it as a tool to reach the masses more effectively.

I can remember how frustrated I felt as a young man thinking about evangelizing the unsaved. "Lord, there are millions of people who don't know You. Yet here we sit, Sunday after Sunday, the same people doing the same things. We have to do something."

So several of us began to pray together. "Lord, move us to reach out to the lost. Use us by Your Spirit." Slowly, in my heart and in the hearts of others, a vision began to grow—a vision of winning thousands of people to Christ.

Some of my own dreams were so wild I didn't tell anyone but my mother about them, and I didn't tell her all of them. She encouraged us, saying, "Come on, you don't need a special message from the Lord before moving out to reach the lost. He gave the order centuries ago to preach the Good News to everyone. So go. Don't keep waiting for more instructions."

So we began to evangelize slowly in a small way. Now I'm amazed when I realize how the Lord has already fulfilled so many of our biggest dreams. "Praise the Lord" is all we can say. "It really happened by His power."

Of course, we must continually recognize God's role in our planning. Psalm 127:1 reminds us, "Unless the Lord builds the house, its builders labor in vain"—no matter how nice a job the architect did on the blueprints.

I believe God encourages us to make plans based on wise and godly counsel. As you read Isaiah, for instance, you will notice that while God condemns the schemes of the wicked (30:1), He commends the plans of the upright (32:8)—even though He ordained everything long ago (37:26).

Our planning is never intended to replace God's sovereign leading in our lives. Paul demonstrated this in his own ministry. Yes, he had a definite strategy for letting all the Roman Empire hear the voice of God, but he was not bound to his plans. He remained sensitive to the Spirit's leading. Remember how the Spirit compelled Him to go to Macedonia, for example, even though he had other plans (Acts 16:6-10).

This is an exciting concept to me. On the one hand, God intends for us to use logical, strategic planning in fulfilling the Great Commission. But on the other hand, God can redirect our plans when necessary. One doesn't necessarily cancel out the need for the other.

Do you have dreams and plans of what God might do through your life? Or are you just busy with life's routine, ordinary tasks? Have you become bored—or boring?

The Lord Jesus Christ challenges us to abandon our complacency when He says, "You can do even greater things than I have done through my Spirit who indwells you." He doesn't intend for us to sit idly and simply dream of what could happen for His glory. He wants us to plan great plans so that those dreams can come true!

William Carey upset the status quo of the church in his day when he proposed sending missionaries from Britain to evangelize other parts of the world. Older Christians told him to give up his preposterous ideas. Carey countered their boredom and doubt by writing, "Expect great things from God, attempt great things for God." That statement became the creed of the modern missions movement as men and women followed Carey's example and went to the ends of the earth with the saving message of Christ's Gospel. Like Carey, God wants us to attempt great things for Him to reach our generation.

Over the years God has stretched my own vision. At first, God burdened my heart for the city of Cordoba where I lived as a young man, then neighboring areas, then all of Argentina. Finally, I dreamed of preaching the Gospel throughout all of Latin America.

But God wasn't through with me yet. Today, in faith, our evangelistic association wants to let the whole world hear the voice of God. With that dream, we are planning massive crusades, multiplied by radio and television, to reach large segments of the world's population. And by God's grace, as partners in evangelism with other Christians and their churches and organizations, we are seeing thousands of lives changed!

What about you? Are you expecting great things from God? Or are you letting the opportunities pass you by? If it's true that the Lord wants the Gospel preached worldwide, then we can't remain passive. Whatever our gifts or abilities or resources, we need to work together as faithful stewards of what God has bestowed on us.

Dream a little. Envision the 190 million Americans who have not accepted the Gospel in this generation. Many have never even heard it clearly explained. What are you going to do about it?

Start doing something by making specific plans of action. Determine how God could use you to share Christ at work, at school, in your neighborhood—and beyond. Remember, God wants to use you. Let Him!

PRAY GREAT PRAYERS

Years ago I read about this amazing invention called "television" in *Time* magazine and dreamed about how it could be used to broadcast the Gospel to literally millions of people. Little did I realize how effective this tool would become in our mass evangelistic crusades.

Now we often arrange for an hour of broadcasting time after each evening rally. We invite listeners to call us at the local TV station and discuss their problems which often include alcoholism, divorce, immorality, and parent-child conflicts. Many callers end up committing their lives to Christ while on the air.

A wealthy friend of mine who loves the Lord is excited about reaching people through television. Some years ago he told me, "Luis, any time you have an evangelistic campaign overseas, I'll pay for one night of broadcasting. If I can, I'll pay for two or three nights."

It's nice to have friends like that! But to be honest with you, I had the hardest time calling him. So every once in a while he called me. "Hey, don't you have any crusades going? You haven't called me. Don't you need any money?"

Well, of course we have campaigns going, and of course we need money to broadcast the Gospel. But for some reason I was very hesitant to call him.

We're like that with the Lord, too. You see, the Lord doesn't simply tell us to dream great dreams and plan great plans. He adds, "And I will do whatever you ask in my name, so that the Son may bring glory to the Father. You may ask me for anything in my name, and I will do it" (John 14:13-14).

The Lord wants us to ask Him for anything in His

name. *Anything!* He says it not once, but twice. "Look," He says, "I'm going to repeat Myself so that you will know I mean it. Go ahead and pray great prayers and watch Me make it happen."

Like other promises throughout Scripture, this one comes with a condition. "And I will do whatever you ask in my name," and note these words, "so that the Son may *bring glory to the Father.*" That's the key. If we ask so that the Father will be glorified, He'll answer. That's why we can rest assured when we pray for the opportunities and the resources needed to call others to Christ that God won't let us down. He takes delight in answering our petitions.

When my youngest son Stephen was only six years old, like all other boys that age, he had a million requests. He asked me for some of the craziest things. Yet I loved to have him come and ask me anyway. Some of his requests were too much, of course, but I didn't mind. Generally, if I could afford what he wanted, I gave it to him. He's my son.

Our heavenly Father also wants us to come to Him with our requests. And He loves to answer us. Christ said it best when He explained, "If you, then, though you are evil, know how to give good gifts to your children, how much more will your Father in heaven give good gifts to those who ask him!" (Matthew 7:11).

"I will do whatever you ask. . . ." I have claimed that promise many times during my life. One of my first requests was for a coin for a bus ride to work in Argentina. God didn't miraculously drop a coin out of heaven, but He did supply a ride in an unusual way.

God has continued to answer many prayers—prayers for big decisions, desperate needs, safety, personnel, wisdom. Answers to those prayers, whether big or small, have caused my faith to grow and grow.

While we were planning a crusade in Nicaragua several years ago, God demonstrated His willingness to answer our greatest prayers. At first, the budget for the mass evangelistic effort allowed only for limited radio coverage of the meetings. That was enlarged to become a satellite radio network reaching twenty Spanish-speaking countries. Then someone suggested, "Why don't we use television, too? Blanket the entire continent!"

As the magnitude of that vision for reaching two hundred million Spanish-speaking people with the Gospel at one time—and the implications of what it could cost—hit us, with one accord we went to our knees before the Lord. In prayer we committed the immense undertaking to God and asked Him to supply the finances we needed. We rose from our knees confident that He would provide.

And He did! When the bills were in and the accounting completed, the needed two hundred thousand dollars had come in, almost to the penny!

A year later we again enlarged our vision for evangelism and asked the Lord for half a million dollars. It seemed like a ridiculous amount for a bunch of missionaries to request. Still, we believed the Lord would provide.

But then I had second thoughts. Oh, I still wanted the Lord to meet our financial needs, but I couldn't bring myself to come right out with John 14:13-14 in front of me and say, "Lord Jesus, You told me to ask for anything, and I'm asking you for five hundred thousand dollars."

Instead, I began to "sell" the Lord on our vision. I whittled it down, saying, "Lord, if You could send twenty thousand dollars this month, because we're having a crusade in Mexico, and then next month if You could send . . ."

Suddenly I realized, "How stupid! The Lord knows all

our plans. I'm not going to break any news to Him if I tell Him we need half a million dollars."

Christ said, "I will do whatever you ask in my name." Whatever we ask! He doesn't say, "Sell Me on your idea; convince Me that I should give you what you want." He merely says, "Ask."

I confessed to the Lord my disobedience and asked Him for half a million dollars, and He provided again!

OBEY GREAT COMMANDS

The Lord Jesus Christ has been calling His disciples to gain a vision for evangelism. He's encouraged them to dream great dreams, plan great plans, and pray great prayers. But that's not all.

Christ offers one further word of encouragement when He adds, "If you love me, you will obey what I command" (John 14:15).

At first glance, His statement seems out of place. Unlike the preceding three verses in John 14 that we've considered, this one isn't a promise. Or is it?

The context of this passage gives us a clue. In verse 21 we read, "Whoever has my commands and obeys them, he is the one who loves me. He who loves me will be loved by my Father, and I too will love him and show myself to him." In other words, we experience God's love when we obey His commands. That's a promise worth remembering!

The value of doing what we have been told—for our own good—was illustrated vividly for me in early 1983 when more than ninety people conducted an all-night search for an eight-year-old boy named Dominic. While on a skiing trip with his father, this little boy apparently had ridden a new lift and skied off the run without realizing it. They hoped to find Dominic somewhere on the snowy mountain slope before it was too late.

As each hour passed, the search party and the boy's family became more and more concerned. By dawn they still had found no trace of him. Two helicopters joined the search, and within fifteen minutes they spotted ski tracks. A ground team followed the tracks, which changed to small footprints. The footprints led to a tree where they found the boy at last.

"He's in super shape," Sgt. Terry Silbaugh, area search and rescue coordinator, announced to the anxious family and press. "In fact, he's in better shape than we are right now." A hospital spokesman said the boy was in fine condition and wasn't even admitted.

Silbaugh explained why the boy did so well despite spending a night in the freezing elements. His father had enough forethought to warn the boy what to do if he became lost, and his son had enough trust to do exactly what his father said.

Dominic protected himself from possible frostbite and hypothermia by snuggling up to a tree and covering himself with branches. As a young child he never would have thought of doing this on his own. He was simply obeying his wise and loving father.[2]

Dominic reminds me of what we should do as children of our loving and wise heavenly Father. We are not to walk according to the course of this world that is passing away. Instead, we are to walk in obedience to the Lord's commands. After all, He knows what is best for us. That's one of the reasons I believe the Bible is so relevant for us today. It gives us God's commands.

The Apostle Peter talks about this near the beginning of his first letter. He tells us, "As obedient children, do not conform to the evil desires you had when you lived in ignorance.

But just as he who called you is holy, so be holy in all you do; for it is written: 'Be holy, because I am holy'" (1 Peter 1:14-16).

You might be thinking, *But isn't Peter—impulsive, denying Peter—being a bit idealistic? How does he really expect us to achieve such obedience and holiness while here on earth?*

Some Christians feel they can attain to Peter's exhortation if they work hard enough and pray long enough. But that's the essence of legalism. As sincere as a legalist may be, if he is relying on his own power and not on the indwelling Christ, then he is heading for a terrible fall.

That was the case with Moses when he killed the Egyptian who had been beating a Hebrew slave. Moses was sincere in his intentions, but he was relying on his own power, the weapons of the flesh.

This was my own situation when I came to the United States in 1961 to further my biblical studies at Multnomah School of the Bible. I had big dreams that I wanted to see quickly accomplished. My impatience led me to rely on my own power, not the Lord's.

During one of the last chapel services at school before the end of the term, our speaker was Major Ian Thomas, founder of the Torchbearers in England. Major Thomas's theme was, "Any Old Bush Will Do, As Long As God Is in the Bush."

He pointed out that it took Moses forty years in the wilderness to get to the point that he was nothing. God was trying to tell Moses, "I don't need a pretty bush or an educated bush or an eloquent bush. Any old bush will do, as long as I am in the bush. If I am going to use you, I am going to use you. It will not be you doing something for Me, but Me doing something through you."

Major Thomas suggested that the bush in the desert was likely a dry bunch of ugly little sticks that had hardly developed, yet Moses had to take off his shoes. Why? Because this was holy ground. Why? Because God was in the bush!

I was like that bush. I could do nothing for God. All my reading, studying, asking questions, and trying to model myself after others was worthless. Everything in my ministry was worthless unless God was in me! No wonder I felt so frustrated. Only He could make something happen.

When Major Thomas closed with Galatians 2:20, it all came together. "I have been crucified with Christ and I no longer live, but Christ lives in me. The life I live in the body, I live by faith in the Son of God, who loved me and gave himself for me."

I realized that the secret to being an obedient, holy Christian was depending on the indwelling, resurrected, almighty Lord Jesus, and not on myself. God was finally in control of this bush!

I had tremendous peace because I realized I didn't have to struggle to be holy. How sad that I had wasted eight years of my life trying to do everything in my own power.

But just because we cannot work to become holy—any more than we can work for our salvation—doesn't mean we should quench the Spirit and do nothing!

Christians who sit still or stand around when God wants them acting, speaking, and moving remind me of Bill Fuqua. In case you haven't heard about him, Fuqua is the current *Guinness Book of World Records* champion at doing nothing. He appears so absolutely still during his routines at shopping malls, fairgrounds, and amusement parks that he's sometimes mistaken for a mannequin.

Fuqua discovered his unique talent at the age of fourteen while standing motionless in front of a Christmas tree as a joke. A woman touched him and exclaimed, "Oh, I thought it was a real person."

Do people question whether you're a real Christian or not? If you are a true disciple of Christ, you will willingly and eagerly obey the Lord Jesus' great commands.

After all, the first step in the Christian life is confessing "Jesus as Lord" (Romans 10:9). Indeed, the day is coming when "every tongue shall confess that Jesus Christ is Lord" (Philippians 2:11). Why? Because God the Father has given Him supremacy over all creation (Colossians 1:18). Christ is the very "King of kings and Lord of lords" (1 Timothy 6:15).

Every subsequent step in the Christian life involves obeying Jesus as Lord. The Apostle John tells us, "We know that we have come to know him if we obey his commands" (1 John 2:3). To the degree that we know and believe that Jesus is Lord, to that degree we obey Him. The Bible calls this "the fear of the Lord."

The fear of the Lord implies a deep reverence and awe of God—and a corresponding response of obedience. Psalm 112:1 says, "Blessed is the man who fears the LORD, who finds great delight in his commands."

Christ knew that the obedience of His disciples depended on their conviction that He was—and is—the Lord. That's why He began His last words to them after His resurrection with the declaration, "All authority in heaven and on earth has been given to me" (Matthew 28:18). Because He is the Lord of lords, He has every right to issue great commands.

Then Christ adds, "Therefore go and make disciples of all nations, baptizing them in the name of the Father and of the Son and of the Holy Spirit, and teaching them to obey everything I have commanded" (Matthew 28:19-20). We often think of this as the Great Commission. But actually His commands are always great. He never gives little, puny suggestions.

Because of the great commands we have received from

Christ, our vision as Christians should be to win as many people as possible to Jesus Christ throughout the world.

Investment advisor Austin Pryor tells how God changed his priorities. "As I began to get more burdened about the Great Commission, business concerns couldn't compete. Let's say you're a marketing person: You can either spend your life trying to get more people to drink Coke, or you can spend your life trying to help fulfill the Great Commission. There's no comparison. It captures your imagination, your affections, your energies. You want to invest in it. I began to feel that commodities trading wasn't important enough for me to be spending that much time on. Eventually, it fell by the wayside."[3]

Evangelism is not an option in the Christian life. Paul admitted, "Yet when I preach the gospel, I cannot boast, for I am compelled to preach. Woe to me if I do not preach the gospel!" (1 Corinthians 9:16).

THE GREATEST THRILL

The day came in my own life when I decided I didn't have the gift of evangelism. It was obvious. I had been zealously preaching the Gospel in Argentina, but no one was coming to Christ. Nothing I did seemed to make a difference. I was inspired by the things I read and heard about Billy Graham's ministry, but I knew I didn't have whatever he had.

I gave God a deadline: "If I don't see any converts through my preaching by the end of the year, I'm quitting." Oh, I would still be an obedient Christian, I thought, but I would bypass the Great Commission and other verses and resign myself simply to teaching other believers.

The end of the year came and went. No converts. My mind was made up; I was through evangelizing. Now I was sure I didn't have the gift.

On Saturday morning, about four days into the new year, the small church I attended held a home Bible study. I didn't feel like going but went anyway out of loyalty to the elders.

The fellow who was supposed to lead the Bible study didn't come. So the man of the house said, "Luis, you are going to have to say something." I was completely unprepared.

I had been reading a book, however, by Billy Graham called *The Secret of Happiness*. It was based on the Beatitudes. So I asked for a New Testament and read Matthew 5:1-12. Then I simply repeated whatever I remembered from Billy Graham's book.

As I was commenting on the beatitude, "Blessed are the pure in heart, for they shall see God," a lady suddenly stood. She began to cry and said, "My heart is not pure. How can I see God? Somebody tell me how I can get a pure heart." How delightful it was to lead her to Jesus Christ!

I don't remember the woman's name, but I will never forget her words: "Somebody tell me how I can get a pure heart." We went to the Bible and read, "The blood of Jesus, his [God's] Son, purifies us from all sin" (1 John 1:7). Before the evening was over, that woman found peace with God, and she went home with a pure heart overflowing with joy.

The greatest joy comes from winning people to Jesus Christ. Your graduation is exciting. Your wedding day is exciting. Your first baby is exciting. But the most thrilling thing you can ever do is win someone to Christ. And, you know, it's contagious. Once you do it, you don't want to stop.

I challenge you to pray, "Oh, Lord, I want that experience. I want to know what it is to win someone to Jesus Christ."

Are you willing to gain a vision of what God could do through you to win others to Himself? After all, God doesn't have a Plan A, a Plan B, and a Plan C for evangelizing the world. He has only one plan—and that's you and me.[4]

TO PONDER

1. Read John 14:12-15 again. What is Jesus asking us to believe? What is He calling us to do?

2. "Jesus calls us to dream great dreams of what we can do to impact the world for His glory." What is the twofold reason the Lord urges us to have such dreams? Why is it that so few Christians ever accomplish great things for Christ? Where have your own dreams stopped? What do you need to confess?

3. "Paul wasn't content to saturate one small area with the Gospel at the expense of the rest of the world. He had a strategy for reaching the entire Roman Empire." In a nutshell, what was Paul's strategy? How much did he pour into such strategic plans? What does Scripture say God thinks of such great plans?

4. "The Lord wants us to ask Him for anything in His name. *Anything.* He says it not once, but twice. 'Look,' He says, 'I'm going to repeat Myself so that you will know I mean it. Go ahead and pray great prayers and watch Me make it happen.'" This promise comes with what condition? Have you ever claimed this promise? How have you seen God work in answer to your prayers?

5. "We experience God's love when we obey His commands. That's a promise worth remembering!" Why is it in our own best interest to obey God's great commands? Does God really expect us to live consistently holy and godly lives this side of heaven? If so, by what power?

6. "Evangelism is not an option in the Christian life." After all, Jesus Christ *commanded* us to "make disciples." But why do so many Christians resist obeying this command? Why does it seem so hard to even try to evangelize others?

7. "The most thrilling thing you can ever do is win someone to Christ. And, you know, it's contagious. Once you do it, you don't want to stop." Have you had that experience yet? If not, are you willing to gain a vision of what God could do through you to win others to Himself? If you don't fervently pray for and then evangelize those you know and love who haven't yet trusted Christ, who will?

Bonus: One very effective tool for presenting the Gospel to an unsaved friend or family member is the booklet *What Is a Real Christian?* The text is featured as an appendix to this book. For a beautiful full-color edition to give away, free of charge, please write to me today. My address appears on page 191.

WHAT IS A REAL CHRISTIAN?

Here is the text of one of my best-known gospel messages, which I've had the privilege of presenting in crusades and booklet form to more than six million people in thirty-two languages. It's not perfect, by any means, but it shows how to take people where they are, get past their misconceptions, present the gospel basics, and then call for a commitment to Jesus Christ.

DID YOU KNOW THAT four out of five Americans today consider themselves Christians? That's the latest word from pollster George Gallup, Jr.

But what Gallup didn't ask was: What does it take to make someone a real Christian? Most likely, ten out of ten Americans would answer that question differently.

I'm convinced that most Americans are as confused about this crucial issue as I once was. Like many others, I grew up attending Sunday school and church. I knew a lot of songs and stories. But I wasn't a Christian.

Oh, if someone had asked me, I could stand up and quote a few Bible verses. I could even say a prayer if you asked me to do so. But for several years I went through a lot of empty religious motions until someone helped me settle the question of whether I was really a Christian.

God wants each of us to know where we stand in His eyes. That's why I believe it isn't mere chance that you have this book in your hands.

Ask yourself, "Am I a real Christian?" You can know for sure!

WHAT IS A REAL CHRISTIAN?

"Don't worry about me," my grandfather insisted as he lay dying in a Buenos Aires hospital. I sat at his bedside, urging him to put his trust in God.

My grandfather put me off, insisting, "I'm all right. After all, I'm Scotch-Presbyterian." He had been born near Edinburgh, Scotland, but since moving to Argentina had definitely preferred scotch to Presbyterian. He loved scotch on the rocks, but the Presbyterian thing he didn't care for much at all.

He died later that same day, believing one of the many popular myths about what makes someone a real Christian.

Maybe you were raised in a Catholic or Protestant home. Or maybe you were brought up in some other religion. And you tell yourself, "Well, I think I'm all right. Don't worry about me." No matter what your background, I encourage you to take an honest look—beyond the myths—about what makes someone a Christian.

Myth #1:
Being Born in America Makes You a Christian

I've met people who have told me, "I was born in America, so of course I am a Christian. What do you take me to be—a heathen?" The truth is that they could be a lot of things.

Others have said: "I've been a Christian all my life; I was born in a Christian home" or "in the church." But since when does where you're born determine what you are? As one of my friends quipped, someone may be born in a stable, but that doesn't make him a horse. Nor does being born in an airport make someone an airplane.

Be thankful for where you were born and for the family and church in which you were reared. But don't assume that automatically makes you a Christian. God has no grandchildren.

Myth #2:
Thinking Positively Makes You a Christian

Some people also think that if you give a hearty handshake, pat others on the back, smile, and ask, "How are you doing?" that you're somehow a Christian.

Now, normally a Christian is cheerful and excited about life and genuinely cares about others. A Christian also understands that he or she is valuable in God's eyes because He made us and loves us deeply.

But you could develop a certain sense of well-being and self-worth apart from knowing what God's Word, the Bible, teaches us about thinking right in an unright world. So thinking positively about life in general and about yourself in particular doesn't automatically make you a Christian.

Myth #3:
Living a Good Life Makes You a Christian

And, then, living a clean and moral life doesn't make anyone a Christian. Many atheists live decent, straight lives. Anyway, how good is "good"? That is the real issue. Most people have a warped idea of the true standard against which our goodness should be measured.

Compared to a mass murderer, you may feel that you're ready for sainthood. Even compared with your family and friends, you may come out okay.

But God's standard of goodness is very different. He puts you up against His Son, Jesus Christ, who lived an absolutely perfect life here on earth. Compared with this level of perfection, our own goodness looks pretty shabby.

Remember, the world has always had plenty of "good" people. So if goodness were enough, God need not have sent Jesus. The fact that Jesus had to come to die on the cross to make our forgiveness possible shows that goodness doesn't make someone a Christian.

Myth #4:
Going to Church Makes You a Christian

Last Sunday four out of ten Americans went to church. But does that mean that all these people are Christians? Of course not. Even some thieves go to church.

Some people go to church because it's a social habit. Others attend because their family makes them go. At the encouragement of a minister, they may even go to special classes for confirmation or membership.

It is true that Christians go to church and take an active part in church life. But attending church doesn't make you a Christian.

Myth #5:
Giving to Others Makes You a Christian

Many of us were taught since childhood to give a portion

of our income to charity or to the church. Whether rich or poor, we feel it's our "Christian" duty.

Even Prince Charles, heir to the British throne, says he feels a "duty to do something" so that "in some way I can make life a little less stinking for some people." So he donates part of his wealth to worthy causes. And that's commendable. But that's not what makes somebody a Christian.

Yes, Christians give to others. More than anyone else, they help the needy and less fortunate. But you can give away everything you own and still not be a Christian.

Myth #6:
Receiving a Sacrament Makes You a Christian

Maybe you were baptized as a child or young adult. That doesn't necessarily mean you're a Christian. Many violent inmates in penitentiaries were baptized years ago. But few people would consider these inmates Christians.

Or maybe you take Communion every Sunday. If you're a Christian, that's great. But I've had someone tell me, "Mr. Palau, I'm confused. I take Communion every week, but I don't know what it means to be a Christian."

You see, both baptism and Communion are biblical. God commands Christians to observe these ordinances. But receiving either one won't make you a Christian.

Myth #7:
Believing in God Makes You a Christian

Eight out of ten people in America say they believe God exists. But are they all Christians? Colonel James Irwin, remembered for his Apollo 15 moon mission, told me that while he was in the Middle East, a Muslim leader said to him, "You talk about God so much—why aren't you a Muslim?"

Do you see my point? If you can be a Muslim and believe in God, then it is not "believing in God" that makes you a Christian.

I have a good friend who believes in exercise. But he never does any. He is forty-five pounds overweight and hopelessly out of shape.

I know countless small boys who believe in soap. But they are not a shade cleaner in spite of their belief.

Belief, on its own, makes no difference. That is why belief, by itself, doesn't make someone a Christian.

Myth #8:
Talking About Jesus Christ Makes You a Christian

Many people talk about Jesus Christ and even speak well of Him. They may be teachers, ministers, church leaders, or "just plain folk." But they may not even believe that the Bible's message about Jesus is true.

Some actually have a distorted view of Jesus that fits their own way of thinking, rather than seeing the Jesus of history and the Bible. And that disqualifies them from calling themselves real Christians.

Myth #9:
Praying Makes You a Christian

Certainly Christians pray. But someone can pray and still not be a Christian. Hindus pray all the time. Muslims pray five times a day.

When traveling abroad, the late Egyptian President Anwar Sadat carried a little prayer rug on which to kneel five times daily. But he was a Muslim, not a Christian. So praying in itself doesn't make someone a Christian.

Myth #10:
Reading the Bible Makes You a Christian

Of course Christians love the Bible. Some of us read it daily. But just reading the Bible doesn't mean you are a Christian.

When Karl Marx was seventeen years old, he wrote a fantastic explanation of part of John's gospel in the New Testament portion of the Bible.[1] Great theologians agree with much of what he said. But Karl Marx eventually rejected the Bible's authority, and during his adult life he called himself an atheist, a Communist—anything but a Christian.

Nikita Khrushchev, the former premier of the USSR, read the Bible when he was a boy. Yet later he made it his ambition to bury the church in the Soviet Union by 1965. Instead, he is buried, and the Russian church continues to grow.

Read the Bible all you can. It explains how to settle this issue once and for all. Since it's God's Word, not man's, we can trust it completely. But remember, just reading the Bible won't make you a Christian.

WHAT MAKES YOU A REAL CHRISTIAN?

"Luis," you may be wondering by now, "if I can't be born a Christian, and if thinking positively, living morally, going to church, giving to others, receiving a sacrament, believing in God, talking about Jesus, praying, and reading the Bible don't make me a Christian, then what does? What is a real Christian?"

Let me mention three basic principles from God's Word

that describe a real Christian. Then I'll explain how today you can become a real Christian.

Walking in the Way of Life

First of all, the Bible says that a Christian is *someone who walks in the way of life* rather than the way of death. That way to life is found in Jesus Christ, the Son of God.

Jesus said, "I am the way and the truth and the life. No one comes to the Father except through me" (John 14:6). Notice that Jesus does not say he will *show* you the way. He says, "I *am* the way!"

Jesus also spoke of a narrow road and a wide road. Many walk on that wide road, which in the end is the way of death (see Matthew 7:13).

Do you sometimes feel as though you are lost and don't know where you are going? When you become a Christian, you have found the way of life.

You ask, "What kind of way is this way of life?"

It is the way of *peace*. God's peace fills your heart when you walk in the way of Christ. Jesus said to His followers, "Peace I leave with you; my peace I give you. I do not give to you as the world gives" (John 14:27). God's peace is a gift available to each of us.

When you walk in the way of Christ, you experience an inner peace—tremendous quiet in your heart. The broken pieces in your life are put together again. Oh, the psychiatrist can analyze you. The psychologist can pinpoint some of the problems in your past. But only God can give you lasting peace.

The way of life is also the way of *purity*. The Bible says, "Blessed are the pure in heart, for they will see God" (Matthew 5:8).

If you are fooling around with sin; if you are playing with

immorality; if you are not being truthful in your business; if you are dishonest in your school, in your work, in your play, in your home—then you know nothing of the way of life.

You may consider yourself a nice person, perhaps the life and soul of the party. But you are not a Christian, because the way of Christ is the way of purity.

When you come to Christ, He forgives your sins and purifies your heart. That doesn't mean you suddenly become holier than everyone else. On the contrary, you become more conscious of your shortcomings. But God gives you the power to live a righteous life.

The way of life in Christ is also the way of *love*. "By this all men will know that you are my disciples, if you love one another," Jesus said (John 13:35). The Bible adds, "We know that we have passed from death to life, because we love our brothers" (1 John 3:14).

Today the word *love* has been robbed of meaning. It's used to describe a person exploiting the emotions of another for his own satisfaction and selfishness. But that is not love. True love wants the very best for someone no matter what it may cost us.

The way of life is also the way of *obedience*. The way of the Christian is to serve only one master—Jesus. The Bible describes Him as "Lord of lords and King of kings" (Revelation 17:14). The Christian lives as though this is true. Jesus becomes your Lord, your Master, your King. What He says goes.

The servant of a king waits for the slightest hint of a command and then rushes to obey. A soldier following the leadership of a great commander willingly obeys every order.

Similarly, real Christians give God complete authority over their lives. We will go wherever He wants us to go, do whatever He wants us to do. And we do not care what it may cost in terms of comfort or reputation.

Jesus has every right to rule like that. Remember, He is not supreme because He inherited authority from His ancestors like an earthly king or lord. Nor does He rule like a corrupt military dictator, by using great power to destroy.

Jesus is Lord and King because He made us, He gave His life for us and our sins, and He always does what is best for us.

Enjoying Eternal Life

Second, a Christian is *someone who enjoys eternal life.* He has a more full and complete life. Jesus said, "I have come that they may have life, and have it to the full" (John 10:10).

Life with Christ was not only God's original design for us; it is the way He intends for us to live *today.* That is what makes life with Christ abundant.

And eternal life never ends. It goes beyond physical death—forever and ever.

Do you have eternal life? You may say, "Well, I'm not sure."

If I asked if you were married, would you say, "I think so"? Or suppose I asked if you are pregnant. Would you say, "A little bit"? Of course not! These are things you can be absolutely sure about.

Do you know that you have eternal life? If you're already a Christian, you know it. Jesus said concerning those who follow Him in faith: "I give them eternal life, and they shall never perish; no one can snatch them out of my hand" (John 10:28). Do you have that triple security?

First He says, "I give them eternal life."

Second He says, "They shall never perish."

Third, "No one can snatch them out of my hand."

What more could you want? A Christian is someone who discovers these three things to be true.

The Bible also says, "He who has the Son has life" (1 John 5:12). In other words, eternal life is Christ in your heart. Can you say, "Yes, I know I have eternal life. I can remember when Christ came into my heart"?

Becoming God's Child

Furthermore, a Christian is *someone who has been born into God's family* and therefore has become one of God's children. You say, "Luis, I thought everyone was a child of God. Isn't God the Father of all mankind?"

According to the Bible, God is the Creator of all people but not the Father of all people. Many people don't even want him to be their Father.

You become a member of God's family by being born into it. The Lord Jesus said, "Unless a man is born again, he cannot see the kingdom of God" (John 3:3). What does that mean?

When you and I were born into the human family, we had no choice about the matter. That's physical birth.

But to become a child of the heavenly Father, you must have a spiritual birth. This happens when we repent of our sins and put our faith and trust in Jesus Christ.

Every year we celebrate our physical birth with parties and gifts. But do you remember your second birth? If not, you must make a decision. Do you want to become a part of God's family by receiving Christ? The Bible says, "To all who received him, to those who believed in his name, he gave the right to become children of God" (John 1:12).

"BUT MY LIFE IS SO BAD!"

A few years ago, while visiting a South American country, I spoke privately with the president, a military man. "Mr. President," I asked, "do you know Jesus Christ?"

The president smiled and said, "Palau, I've led such a hard life that I don't think God wants to know me very much."

"Mr. President, no matter what you've done, Christ died on the cross for you, and He loves you. If you want to know Him, you can meet Him right now."

As we continued to talk, I explained what Christ had done on the cross, how He died to receive the punishment that should be ours for the wrong we have done. I said, "Sir, would you like to receive Christ now?"

He paused and quite seriously said, "If Christ will receive me, I want to become a real Christian."

Right then we bowed our heads and prayed together. This general opened his heart to the Son of God and received Christ into his life.

He thought God would never receive him because of his past. But when we finished praying, he stood and in typical Latin fashion gave me a tremendous hug. "Thank you," he said. "Now I know that Christ has really received me and forgiven me."

WHAT ABOUT YOU?

Have you decided to trust Christ yet? Would you like to know that you have eternal life? Would you like to start walking in the way of Jesus Christ, knowing that you are a child of God and that you are going to heaven?

Let me tell you how you can become a real Christian— right now before you finish reading this book.

JOINING GOD'S FAMILY

First, the Bible teaches that you must admit that your sins have separated you from God. That's what I liked about that South

American president. He readily admitted he was a sinner. In fact, he was so convinced of the evil and rebellion in his life that he felt God would never receive him.

Have you ever owned up to God about those things in your life that hurt Him—selfishness, pride, greed, immorality, and all the rest? Have you ever admitted that you've been walking in the way of death? You see, "the wages of sin is death" (Romans 6:23).

The Bible also says, "All have sinned and fall short of the glory of God" (Romans 3:23). That includes you and me. Is it time to own up to God and to receive the forgiveness that He wants to give you?

Second, you must believe what Christ has done for you on the cross. The Bible says, "Christ died for sins once for all, the righteous for the unrighteous, to bring you to God" (1 Peter 3:18).

When Jesus died on the cross, He conquered death so that each of us may be forgiven. We deserve to be punished for the wrong we have done in God's eyes. But God sent His Son to receive our punishment in His body on the cross (see 1 Peter 2:24).

It is like a judge finding a prisoner guilty, taking the prisoner's place, and receiving the sentence himself. What magnificent love!

"BUT I DON'T UNDERSTAND!"

You may not completely understand how God places the penalty for your sin on His Son. But you do not need to understand everything all at once. God only asks you to believe.

I have been told that no one totally understands electricity. Scientists talk about it as a fundamental element of all matter. They can create electrical charges and harness electricity.

But as a Stanford University scientist once told me, "Electricity in its essence is quite unexplainable."

When you become a real Christian, you may not understand it all at the beginning. But as you read the Bible and allow God to teach you, your understanding will grow.

The final step you must take is to confess Jesus Christ as your Lord. You cannot inherit faith. It's not enough to say, "My father was a fine Christian, and I was brought up in a fine Christian home." That will not make you one of God's children.

Experience Christ for yourself! All of us who belong to Christ had to come for ourselves. Have you come to Him yet? Have you ever made that decision?

You ask, "How?" The Bible says: "If you confess with your mouth, 'Jesus is Lord,' and believe in your heart that God raised him from the dead, you will be saved. For it is with your heart that you believe and are justified, and it is with your mouth that you confess and are saved" (Romans 10:9-10).

The best way I know to make Jesus the Lord of your life is to simply bow your head in prayer, confess your sins to God, by faith open your heart to Christ, believe in Him, and receive Him.

If that's your decision, then tell God now—silently if you wish—right where you are. You may wish to use this prayer: "Heavenly Father, I want to be a real Christian. I realize that my sins have separated me from You. Please forgive me. I believe in what Christ did for me on the cross. I don't completely understand it, but I accept it by faith. I do want to be a child of Yours. Please come into my life, Lord Jesus, and make me Your child right now. I'll follow You and obey You forever. Amen."

To make a record of your decision, write today's date beside your signature on the line below.

_____

AFTER YOU BECAME
A REAL CHRISTIAN

Have you decided to receive the Lord Jesus as your Savior? If so, you've made the most important decision of your life!

You now belong to God's family, and of course you will want to get to know God better. The best way is to read His Word. I suggest you begin with Luke's gospel in the New Testament. Remember that God speaks to us through the Bible. So as you read, look for examples to follow or instructions to obey.

Saturate yourself with the Bible. Your thoughts and emotions will begin to change as you read the Word of God daily.

Second, meet with other Christians. Find a church that believes the Bible, honors Christ, and teaches what a real Christian is. Go to church and talk to the minister. Say, "I received Christ," and see what happens. If the minister doesn't seem interested in helping you grow spiritually, then find some church that can help you.

Third, begin to pray. You talked to the Lord just now. He answered your prayer. He loves you; He's your Father. Since communication is the key to any relationship, your relationship with God can grow only as you talk to Him in prayer.

If you have truly asked the Lord Jesus to become your Savior, you have taken the most important step in your life that's possible. You've begun an exciting journey that only gets better! And now, as your Christian brother, I want to be the first to say—

"Welcome to God's family!"

NOTES

INTRODUCTION

1. The story of Andrew's conversion is told in "Waiting for Andrew" by Luis Palau, *Moody*, July/August 1994, p. 24.

ONE: THE CHURCH'S (FORGOTTEN) NUMBER ONE PRIORITY

1. George Barna, *Evangelism That Works* (Ventura, Calif.: Regal Books, 1995), pp. 35-36. According to a 1994 survey by the Barna Research Group, nine out of ten adults cannot even define the meaning of the Great Commission. "It is one of the defining commands of Jesus, given as a core challenge to all of His followers, and a central element in the stated mission of churches, denominations, and parachurch organizations worldwide. But the typical American adult, who has undoubtedly been exposed to this long-standing challenge many times, has no recollection of the content of the challenge."

2. Three of the most in-depth follow-up studies were conducted by Roy Pointer with Bible Society and Peter Brierley with MARC Europe (two separate studies of Mission to London, 1983-1984) and Henry J. Schmidt (Central California Crusade, 1986-1987).

3. Barna, *Evangelism That Works*, p. 15.

4. Ibid., p. 22.

5. Jim Reapsome, "Capt. O'Grady's Life Line," *Pulse*, July 21, 1995, p. 8.

6. Barna, *Evangelism That Works*, pp. 12-13.

TWO: CHANGING AMERICA FROM THE INSIDE OUT

1. Jerry Jenkins, "Trophies of Grace," *Moody*, May 1995, p. 6.

2. William T. Ellis, *Billy Sunday: The Man and His Message* (Chicago: Moody Press, 1959), pp. 32-33.

3. The story of Maria Benitez-Perez's conversion is told in *Calling*

America and the Nations to Christ by Luis Palau with David Sanford (Nashville: Thomas Nelson Publishers, 1994), pp. 83-89.

4. The story of Rosario Rivera's conversion is told by David Sanford, "God's Revolutionary," *Christian Family,* June 1986, pp. 21-22, and by John Maust, "Rosario Rivera: Reaching Lima's Children," *Missiology,* July 1987, p. 339.

5. Oscar Sherwin, *John Wesley, Friend of the People* (New York: Twayne Publishers, 1961), p. 30.

6. J. Wesley Bready, *England: Before and After Wesley* (London: Hodder and Stoughton, n.d.), p. 19.

THREE: A MESSAGE FOR AMERICA

1. George Barna, *Evangelism That Works* (Ventura, Calif.: Regal Books, 1995), p. 22.

2. "Hispanic" can mean almost anything and therefore sometimes means almost nothing. My grandparents emigrated from France, Scotland, and Spain to Argentina, a South American nation whose sons and daughters are 97 percent from European descent. My reality and some people's Hispanic stereotypes are at complete odds. I'd rather not be labeled, thank you.

3. Colin Powell, *My American Journey* (New York: Random House, 1995), p. 610.

FOUR: THE GOSPEL OF RECONCILIATION

1. This story of racial reconciliation in Fort Worth is told in "Ernie Horn Is an Unlikely Hero" by Luis Palau, *World Vision,* December 1994/January 1995, pp. 12-15.

2. This story about World Missionary Baptist Church is told by Mike Umlandt in "And the Walls Came Tumbling Down," *World Vision,* December 1994/January 1995, p. 14.

FIVE: WHO'S TELLING THE GOSPEL TRUTH?

1. George Barna, *Evangelism That Works* (Ventura, Calif.: Regal Books, 1995), p. 36. He defines "the Gospel" as "the good news

of Jesus' death and resurrection undertaken to save people from their sins."

2. Ibid., pp. 39-40.

SIX: GOOD WORKS AREN'T GOOD ENOUGH

1. George Barna, *Evangelism That Works* (Ventura, Calif.: Regal Books, 1995), p. 38.
2. Ibid., p. 39.

SEVEN: THE FUTURE OF CRUSADE EVANGELISM

1. As stated later in this chapter, *mass evangelism* "is personal evangelism multiplied a thousand times." People don't attend crusade meetings and come to Christ in a vacuum; most come at the invitation of a friend, go forward with that friend, and are spiritually nurtured by that friend and others for months afterward.
2. Russell Chandler, *Racing Toward 2001* (Grand Rapids, Mich.: Zondervan, 1992), p. 310.
3. Letter to Mike Umlandt dated April 26, 1993.
4. The multiplication theory suggests we can win the world to Jesus Christ in a single generation by using a discipleship-oriented approach: one person leads a second person to Christ and disciples him; then the two of them reach two more people, disciple the new converts, then together reach four people, et cetera. I endorse the approach but have to dismiss the theory as untenable. The process inevitably breaks down, often within the first couple of years.
5. "U.S. Crusades Call for Creativity, Prayer, Nerve," *LPEA Heartbeat*, July 1993, pp. 2-3.

EIGHT: GOD'S OBSESSION

1. Richard Hoffer and Shelley Smith, "Putting His House in Order," *Sports Illustrated*, January 16, 1995, pp. 28-32.
2. For a full account of this life-changing discovery, read *Say Yes! How to Renew Your Spiritual Passion* (Grand Rapids, Mich.: Discovery House Publishers, 1995).

3. Granted, not all evangelists are zealous. Some may be neglecting other God-given duties. Service for God is no excuse to avoid other responsibilities, priorities, or obligations.

4. "The Cost of Loving Jesus," *Christianity Today*, May 12, 1989, p. 45.

5. This chapter is adapted from Luis Palau's article, "Zeal," *Moody*, September 1995, pp. 24-25.

TEN: DREAM GREAT DREAMS

1. Ray Stedman, *From Guilt to Glory*, Vol. 2 (Waco, Tex.: Word Books, 1978), p. 173.

2. *The Oregonian*, March 15, 1983.

3. "The Cost of Loving Jesus," *Christianity Today*, May 12, 1989, p. 45.

4. This chapter is adapted from Luis Palau's "Dream Great Dreams" message, originally published in booklet form by Multnomah Press.

APPENDIX: WHAT IS A REAL CHRISTIAN?

1. Karl Marx, "On the Union of Believers in Christ," *Decision*, August 1961, pp. 8-9. A copy of the German original, written in August 1835, is among the British Museum's collected works of Marx.

BIBLIOGRAPHY

Alexander, John W. *Believing and Obeying Jesus Christ: The Urbana '79 Compendium*. Downers Grove, Ill.: InterVarsity Press, 1980.

Allen, Roland. *The Ministry of the Spirit*. Grand Rapids, Mich.: Wm. B. Eerdmans Publishing Company, 1960.

———. *Missionary Methods: St. Paul's or Ours?* Grand Rapids, Mich.: Wm. B. Eerdmans Publishing Company, 1962.

———. *Missionary Principles*. Grand Rapids, Mich.: Wm. B. Eerdmans Publishing Company, 1964.

———. *The Spontaneous Expansion of the Church*. Grand Rapids, Mich.: Wm. B. Eerdmans Publishing Company, 1962.

Barna, George. *Evangelism That Works*. Ventura, Calif.: Regal Books, 1995.

Bergin, G. Fred, comp. *Autobiography of George Muller,* 3rd ed. London: J. Nisbet and Company, 1914.

Berkley, James D., ed. *Leadership Handbooks of Practical Theology, Volume Two, Outreach and Care*. Grand Rapids, Mich.: Baker Book House, 1994.

Bonar, Andrew A. *Memoir and Remains of Robert Murray M'Cheyne*. Edinburgh: The Banner of Truth Trust, 1973. First published in 1844.

Bonar, Horatius. *Authentic Records of Revival*. Wheaton, Ill.: Richard Owen Roberts Publishers, 1980. First published in 1860 by J. Nisbet and Company, London.

Bready, J. Wesley. *England: Before and After Wesley*. London: Hodder and Stoughton, n.d.

Brown, Elijah P. *The Real Billy Sunday*. Dayton, Ohio: Otterbein Press, 1914.

Burns, James. *The Laws of Revival*. Minneapolis, Minn.: World Wide Publications, 1993.

Chafer, Lewis Sperry. *True Evangelism*. Grand Rapids, Mich.: Zondervan Publishing House, 1967. First published in 1919.

Chandler, Russell. *Racing Toward 2001*. Grand Rapids, Mich.: Zondervan Publishing House, 1992.

Choose Ye This Day. Minneapolis, Minn.: World Wide Publications, 1989.

Coleman, Robert E. *The Master Plan of Evangelism*. Westwood, N.J.: Fleming H. Revell Company, 1964.

Curtis, Richard K. *They Called Him Mister Moody*. Grand Rapids, Mich.: Baker Book House, 1995.

Dallimore, Arnold. *George Whitefield*. London: The Banner of Truth Trust, 1970 (volume 1) and 1979 (volume 2). In the USA, published by Crossway Books, 1990.

Dorsett, Lyle W. *Billy Sunday and the Redemption of Urban America*. Grand Rapids, Mich.: William B. Eerdmans Publishing Company, 1991.

Douglas, J. D., ed. *The Calling of an Evangelist*. Minneapolis, Minn.: World Wide Publications, 1987.

————, ed. *Let the Earth Hear His Voice*. Minneapolis, Minn.: World Wide Publications, 1975.

Edman, V. Raymond. *Finney Lives On*. Minneapolis, Minn.: Bethany Fellowship, 1971.

Ellis, James J. *Charles Haddon Spurgeon*. London: J. Nisbet and Company, n.d.

Ellis, William T. *"Billy" Sunday: The Man and His Message*. Philadelphia: John C. Winston Company, 1914. Later revised and published by Moody Press, 1959.

Ferm, Robert O. *Cooperative Evangelism*. Grand Rapids, Mich.: Zondervan Publishing House, 1958.

Ferm, Robert O., with Caroline M. Whiting. *Billy Graham: Do the Conversions Last?* Minneapolis, Minn.: World Wide Publications, 1988.

Findlay, James F., Jr. *Dwight L. Moody: American Evangelist, 1837-1899*. Chicago: University of Chicago Press, 1969.

Finney, Charles G. *An Autobiography*. Old Tappan, N.J.: Fleming H. Revell Company, n.d. First published as *Memoirs of Charles G. Finney*, 1876.

Fitt, Arthur Percy. *The Shorter Life of D. L. Moody*. Chicago: Moody Press, n.d. First published as Moody, W. R. and A. P. Fitt, *Life of D. L. Moody*, London: Morgan and Scott, n.d. [1900].

Ford, Leighton. *The Christian Persuader*. New York: Harper & Row, Publishers, 1966.

Fountain, Jeff. *The Final Frontier*. Eastbourne, England: Kingsway Publications, 1987.

Getz, Gene. *The Measure of Spiritual Maturity*. Richardson, Tex.: Grace Products Corporation, 1993. Eleven-part video series and workbook.

Gibbs, Alfred P. *The Preacher and His Preaching*. Kansas City, Kan.: Walterick Publishers, n.d.

———. *A Primer on Preaching*. Fort Dodge, Iowa: Walterick Printing Company, n.d.

Graham, Billy. *A Biblical Standard for Evangelists*. Minneapolis, Minn.: World Wide Publications, 1984.

Grasso, Domenico. *Proclaiming God's Message*. Notre Dame, Ind.: University of Notre Dame Press, 1965.

Green, Michael. *Evangelism in the Early Church*. Grand Rapids, Mich.: William B. Eerdmans Publishing Company, 1970.

Hardman, Keith J. *Seasons of Refreshing*. Grand Rapids, Mich.: Baker Book House, 1995.

Henry, Carl F. H., and W. Stanley Mooneyham. *One Race, One Gospel, One Task*, 2 vols. Minneapolis, Minn.: World Wide Publications, 1967. A compendium of the World Congress on Evangelism, Berlin, 1966.

High, Stanley. *Billy Graham*. New York: McGraw-Hill Book Company, 1956.

Holton, Susan, and David L. Jones. *Spirit Aflame*. Grand Rapids, Mich.: Baker Book House, 1985.

Howard, David M., ed. *Declare His Glory*. Downers Grove, Ill.: InterVarsity Press, 1977.

Hughes, Philip Edgcumbe. *Theology of the English Reformers*. London: Hodder and Stoughton, 1965.

Huston, Sterling W. *Crusade Evangelism and the Local Church*. Minneapolis, Minn.: World Wide Publications, 1984.

Johnston, Arthur. *The Battle for World Evangelism*. Wheaton, Ill.: Tyndale Publishing House, 1978.

Johnstone, Patrick. *Operation World*, 5th ed. Grand Rapids, Mich.: Zondervan Publishing House, 1993.

Kennedy, D. James. *Evangelism Explosion*, rev. ed. Wheaton, Ill.: Tyndale House Publishers, 1977.

Latourette, Kenneth Scott. *A History of the Expansion of Christianity*, 7 vols. Grand Rapids, Mich.: Zondervan Publishing House, 1970. First published by Harper & Row, Publishers, 1937-1945.

Lazell, David. *Gipsy Smith: From the Forest I Came*. Chicago: Moody Press, 1973.

Lyall, Leslie T. *John Sung: Flame for God in the Far East*, rev. ed. Chicago: Moody Press, 1964.

Macfarlan, D. *The Revivals of the Eighteenth Century.* Wheaton, Ill.: Richard Owen Roberts Publishers, 1980. First published by Johnston and Hunter, Edinburgh, 1847.

Martin, William. *A Prophet with Honor: The Billy Graham Story.* New York: William Morrow and Company, 1991.

McGavran, Donald Anderson, ed. *Church Growth and Christian Mission.* New York: Harper & Row, Publishers, 1965.

McLeish, James, ed. *Faithful Witness: The Urbana '84 Compendium.* Downers Grove, Ill.: InterVarsity Press, 1985.

Miller, Basil. *Charles G. Finney.* Minneapolis, Minn.: Bethany Fellowship, 1966.

Mitchell, Curtis. *Billy Graham: Saint or Sinner.* Old Tappan, N.J.: Fleming H. Revell Company, 1979.

———. *God in the Garden.* Garden City, N.Y.: Doubleday and Company, 1957.

———. *The Making of a Crusader.* Philadelphia: Chilton Books, 1966.

Moody, William R. *The Life of D. L. Moody.* New York: Fleming H. Revell Company, 1900.

Moody, W. R. and A. P. Fitt. *Life of D. L. Moody.* London: Morgan and Scott, n.d. [1900]. Later published as Fitt, Arthur Percy, *The Shorter Life of D. L. Moody,* Chicago: Moody Press, n.d.

No Stranger in the City. Leicester, England: Inter-Varsity Press, 1989.

Orr, J. Edwin. *The Second Evangelical Awakening,* rev. London: Marshall, Morgan and Scott, 1964.

Packer, J. I. *Evangelism and the Sovereignty of God.* London: Inter-Varsity Fellowship, 1961.

Palau, Luis. *Dream Great Dreams.* Portland, Oreg.: Multnomah Press, 1984.

Palau, Luis, with David Sanford. *Calling America and the Nations to Christ*. Nashville: Thomas Nelson Publishers, 1994.

———. *Healthy Habits for Spiritual Growth*. Grand Rapids, Mich.: Discovery House Publishers, 1994.

———. *Heart for the World*. Manila: OMF Publishers, 1989. Published for the Lausanne II in Manila Congress on World Evangelization.

———. *Renewing Your Spiritual Passion*. Edmonton, Alberta: Crown Video, 1992. Three-part video series.

———. *Say Yes: How to Renew Your Spiritual Passion*. Grand Rapids, Mich.: Discovery House Publishers, 1994.

———. *What Is a Real Christian?* Portland, Oreg.: Multnomah Press, 1985. Published in thirty-two languages worldwide.

Parker, Percy Livingstone. *The Journal of John Wesley*. Chicago: Moody Press, n.d.

Peters, George W. *Saturation Evangelism*. Grand Rapids, Mich.: Zondervan Publishing House, 1970.

Pierson, A. T. *George Müller of Bristol*. London: J. Nisbet and Company, n.d.

Pollock, John. *Billy Graham*. New York: McGraw-Hill Book Company, 1966.

———. *Billy Graham: Evangelist to the World*. San Francisco: Harper & Row, Publishers, 1979.

———. *George Whitefield and the Great Awakening*. Garden City, N.Y.: Doubleday and Company, 1972.

———. *Moody*. Grand Rapids, Mich.: Zondervan Publishing House, 1963. In the UK published as *Moody Without Sankey*, London: Hodder and Stoughton, 1963.

———. *Wilberforce*. New York: St. Martin's Press, 1977.

Revival in Our Time. Wheaton, Ill.: Van Kampen Press, 1950.

Robertson, Darrel M. *The Chicago Revival, 1876*. Metuchen, N.J.: Scarecrow Press, 1989.

Robinson, Haddon. *Biblical Preaching*. Grand Rapids, Mich.: Baker Book House, 1980.

Schaff, Philip. *History of the Christian Church*, 8 vols. Grand Rapids, Mich.: Wm. B. Eerdmans Publishing Company, n.d. First published in 1866.

Scharpff, Paulus. *History of Evangelism*. Grand Rapids, Mich.: William B. Eerdmans Publishing Company, 1966. Translated from 1964 German edition.

Schubert, William E. *I Remember John Sung*. Singapore: Far Eastern Bible College Press, 1976.

Smith, Oswald J. *The Passion for Souls*. London: Marshall, Morgan and Scott, 1950.

————. *The Revival We Need*. London: Marshall, Morgan and Scott, 1940.

Spurgeon, C. H. *The Soul-winner: How to Lead Sinners to the Saviour*. Grand Rapids, Mich.: Wm. B. Eerdmans Publishing Company, 1963.

————. *C. H. Spurgeon: Autobiography, Volume 2*. Edinburgh: The Banner of Truth Trust, 1973. First published 1897-1900 as the last two of four volumes.

————. *Spurgeon—The Early Years*. London: The Banner of Truth Trust, 1967. Originally published 1897-1900 as the first two of four volumes.

Stott, John R. W. *The Cross of Christ*. Leicester, England: Inter-Varsity Press, 1986.

————. *Preacher's Portrait*. Grand Rapids, Mich.: Wm. B. Eerdmans Publishing Company, 1961.

Streett, R. Alan. *The Effective Invitation*. Old Tappan, N.J.: Fleming H. Revell Company, 1984.

Strobel, Lee. *Inside the Mind of Unchurched Harry & Mary.*
Grand Rapids, Mich.: Zondervan Publishing House, 1993.

Strober, Gerald S. *Graham: A Day in Billy's Life.* Garden City,
N.Y.: Doubleday and Company, 1976.

Telford, John. *The Life of John Wesley.* New York: Eaton and
Mains, n.d.

Tracy, Joseph. *The Great Awakening.* Edinburgh: The Banner of
Truth Trust, 1976. First published in 1842.

Triton, A. N. *Whose World.* London: Inter-Varsity Press, 1970.

Tucker, Ruth A. *From Jerusalem to Irian Jaya: A Biographical
History of Christian Missions.* Grand Rapids, Mich.:
Zondervan Publishing House, 1983.

Tuttle, Robert G. *John Wesley: His Life and Theology.* Grand
Rapids, Mich.: Zondervan Publishing House, 1978.

Weakley, Clare George, Jr. *The Nature of Revival.* Minneapolis,
Minn.: Bethany House Publishers, 1987.

Whitefield, George. *George Whitefield's Journals.* Edinburgh: The
Banner of Truth Trust, 1960. First published 1738-1747.

————. *Letters of George Whitefield.* Edinburgh: The Banner of
Truth Trust, 1976. First published as *The Works of George
Whitefield*, 1771.

Wirt, Sherwood Eliot. *Evangelism: The Next Ten Years.* Waco,
Tex.: Word Books, 1978.

Wood, A. Skevington. *The Burning Heart: John Wesley,
Evangelist.* Exeter, England: Paternoster Press, 1967. In the
USA, published by Bethany Fellowship, 1978.

Woodbridge, John, general ed. *More Than Conquerors: Portraits
of Believers from All Walks of Life.* Chicago: Moody Press,
1992.

Wright, Linda Raney. *Christianity's Crisis in Evangelism.*
Gresham, Oreg.: Vision House Publishing, 1995.

CORRESPONDENCE

THANK YOU FOR TAKING THE TIME to read this book. I'd love to hear from you! And I'd be glad to send you our evangelistic association's PROCLAIM! newsletter free of charge, without any obligation on your part.

It would be an encouragement to know you want to work with us to help re-evangelize America, proclaiming the transforming Gospel of Jesus Christ by all available means in our generation. Please write to me today:

> Luis Palau
> Evangelistic Association
> P.O. Box 1173
> Portland, OR 97207

If you are looking for a resource for helping new believers become established in their faith, ask for *Your New Life with Christ* by Luis Palau (also from Crossway Books).